Praise for **JESUS IS** _____.

"Judah Smith is a unique gift to my generation. In *Jesus Is* _____, he will motivate you to let go of your preconceived, limited view of Jesus so you can embrace who He really is in our lives—more real and relevant than we have ever imagined."

—STEVEN FURTICK, LEAD PASTOR,
ELEVATION CHURCH AND AUTHOR OF THE
NEW YORK TIMES BESTSELLER *GREATER*

"There is not another human being on earth whom I know personally who could tackle a book subject like this as well as Judah Smith. To Judah, Jesus is everything. And from that platform he writes this book. I eagerly await its impact in my city, New York City, and beyond . . . It's overdue."

—CARL LENTZ, LEAD PASTOR,
HILLSONG CHURCH, NEW YORK CITY

"As you read through this book you will discover that Jesus is not at all like you thought and so much more than you imagined."

—CHRISTINE CAINE, FOUNDER
OF THE A21 CAMPAIGN

"This book gives any reader—regardless of where they are in their faith walk—the inspiration to redefine and reignite a new relationship with Jesus."

—TOMMY BARNETT, SENIOR PASTOR,
PHOENIX FIRST AND FOUNDER OF THE
LOS ANGELES DREAM CENTER

"This book will set you on a journey of falling even more in love with the unending characteristics of the greatest man who ever lived."

—BRIAN HOUSTON, SENIOR PASTOR,
HILLSONG CHURCH

"Who is Jesus to you? Finding the answer to this question will change your life forever. Judah Smith is on a mission to share the truth about Jesus, and if you are searching to know more, you will find it in *Jesus Is ____.*"

—CRAIG GROESCHEL, SENIOR PASTOR OF
LIFECHURCH.TV AND AUTHOR OF *SOUL DETOX:
CLEAN LIVING IN A CONTAMINATED WORLD*

"If you truly grasp the concept of this book it will change your life. We all have questions about our faith. Judah has a gift of navigating through all the religious rhetoric and sheds light on who God is, in a way I've never seen before. At the end of this book I guarantee you will feel loved by your Creator."

—JASON KENNEDY, E!
NEWS CORRESPONDENT

"This book will inspire you and make you laugh at the same time. It will also challenge and encourage you. As always, with Judah it is all about Jesus."

—NICKY GUMBEL, VICAR OF
HOLY TRINITY BROMPTON AND
PIONEER OF THE ALPHA COURSE

"Why let your past failures hold you back when Jesus has already paid for them? Judah, as a positive force, teaches what he knows, loves, and believes in . . . Jesus. As he'll often say 'I'm a Jesus guy.'"

—RYAN GOOD, STYLIST FOR JUSTIN BIEBER
AND PRODUCER OF TV SHOW *PUNK'D*

JESUS IS _____.

STUDENT EDITION

JESUS IS _____.

DISCOVERING WHO HE IS CHANGES WHO YOU ARE

STUDENT EDITION

JUDAH SMITH

THOMAS NELSON
Since 1798

NASHVILLE   MEXICO CITY   RIO DE JANEIRO

Jesus Is _____. Student Edition

Published in Nashville, Tennessee, by Thomas Nelson. Thomas Nelson is a registered trademark of HarperCollins Christian Publishing, Inc.

Published in association with the literary agency of Fedd & Company, Inc., P.O. Box 341973, Austin, TX 78734.

Thomas Nelson titles may be purchased in bulk for educational, business, fund-raising, or sales promotional use. For information, please e-mail SpecialMarkets@ ThomasNelson.com.

Unless otherwise noted, Scripture quotations are taken from *Holy Bible*, New Living Translation. © 1996. Used by permission of Tyndale House Publishers, Inc., Wheaton, Illinois 60189. All rights reserved.

Scripture quotations marked ESV are from THE ENGLISH STANDARD VERSION. © 2001 by Crossway Bibles, a division of Good News Publishers.

Scripture quotations marked KJV are from THE KING JAMES VERSION of the Bible, public domain.

Scripture quotations marked NKJV are from THE NEW KING JAMES VERSION. © 1982 by Thomas Nelson. Used by permission. All rights reserved.

ISBN: 978-0-7180-2245-7

Library of Congress Cataloging-in-Publication Data

Smith, Judah.
  Jesus is -- : discovering who He is changes who you are / Judah Smith. -- Student edition.
    pages cm
  Undescore mark appears after "Jesus is" in the title.
  1. Jesus Christ--Person and offices. I. Title.
  BT203.S615 2014
  232--dc23

                              2014022191

Printed in the United States of America

14 15 16 17 RRD 6 5 4 3 2 1

*This book is dedicated to the community I have
been privileged to be a part of since I was thirteen,
the City Church. This is our journey.*

Contents

Foreword

by Bubba Watson

Sometimes God takes your life for some crazy twists and turns. That's the story of my life, actually.

In case you haven't heard of me, I'm a professional golfer. If you've ever watched golf, maybe you've seen a guy who uses a pink club. That would be me. Long story, so don't ask. Anyway, besides the pink club thing, I'm best known for having won the Master's Tournament a couple of times (2012 and 2014).

When I first heard the name Judah Smith, my dad was just weeks away from being called home to heaven. My trainer started talking to me about a great young pastor named Judah Smith from Seattle. A few days later, Judah and I connected through Twitter, and then we started communicating back and forth.

Soon after, my dad passed away. He'd been battling cancer

for a while, but nothing prepares you for your dad dying—even when you know it's coming. I was closer to my dad than to just about anyone else. He was my coach on and off the course. It was a rough time.

Judah was quick to send me some encouraging messages from the Bible. It was a heartfelt gesture and really meant the world to me. I had no idea at the time that Judah was going through the very same thing. His dad was fighting cancer too. Just two months after my dad passed, his dad died as well.

I remember what happened next like it was yesterday. Five days after his dad's death, I wrote Judah and asked him if he wanted to come down to my house to play golf. What can I say? Judah's a pastor; he shared Bible verses. I'm a golfer; I shared the green. Judah and his family packed their bags and came for a visit.

Like I said, God takes you for some crazy twists and turns. The only way you can explain my friendship with Judah is that God made it happen. Judah has helped me be stronger in my relationship with Jesus. He has been a great role model in all areas of life. He has helped me be better at asking God for help with decisions and trusting him every day. As our friendship has grown, he has taught me to be a better husband, better dad, better friend, better listener, better everything—except maybe a better golfer!

How does he do it? He just shares Jesus. That's what gets Judah started and keeps him going. He wants to help people meet Jesus and become more like Jesus.

I hope *Jesus Is ____ Student Edition* will help you do exactly that. It's a simple message, but it's the kind of message every one of us needs to hear.

Introduction

I'm thirty-three years old, and I was born and raised in the Pacific Northwest, which means I love coffee and complaining about the weather. I'm a husband, a father of three, and an okay golfer. I'm also a pastor.

That last bit often makes people feel awkward. They try to watch what they say around me, which mostly makes me laugh. They think I can't relate to them. They think I'm always holy, always perfect, and always judging what they do.

That is a stereotype, of course: a false idea of what a pastor is. I'm as human as the next guy. I make mistakes, I tell jokes, and I like to eat food that is terrible for me. Just like you.

Over the last few years, I've been on a journey that has challenged my stereotypes—of myself, of sin and sinners, of Jesus himself. It's hard to describe how much it has changed me, but I do know this: I'll never be the same again.

Christianity isn't what you might think it is. It isn't about not saying bad words, or about not cheating on a test, or about not having bad thoughts. Really, it's not about "not" at all.

Christianity is about Jesus.

The Campaign

About three years ago, soon after becoming the main pastor at my church, I sat down with the media team and told them I wanted to launch a marketing campaign in our city. My goal: to get Jesus on the mind of Seattle.

Christianity IS about JESUS.

I didn't want to promote our church. I didn't want to promote a certain way of living. I just wanted people to think more about Jesus.

Out of that little meeting came the "Jesus Is _____" campaign. We used billboards, bus signs, Facebook ads, bumper magnets (not stickers—people love their cars), and a website, jesus-is.org, where people could fill in the blank themselves. We also organized hundreds of what we called "Jesus Is _____ Projects," where people in our church cleaned up parks, volunteered at schools, and did other community service projects.

If we could get PEOPLE to think about Jesus, JESUS was more than ABLE to show himself to THEM.

The big idea of the campaign was just to get people thinking about Jesus. If we could get people to think about Jesus, Jesus was more than able to show himself to them.

The response was overwhelming. People have visited different pages on our website over one and a half million times. Seventy-five thousand people and counting have submitted answers to the blank.

The campaign has been mentioned on a ton of other websites, both good and bad. Hackers have targeted it multiple times.

Apparently Jesus gets a reaction out of people.

The answers people submit are incredibly moving. The website provides an amazing picture of our world's idea of Jesus. Many submissions, of course, are pro-Jesus. Others are simply funny. Some are bizarre. Many are very anti-Jesus; sometimes they're even hateful.

Our MISSION: to show you who JESUS IS.

Within months of launching the campaign, we realized something. Jesus Is _____ was more than a clever campaign or a marketing approach. It was the mission of our church.

A giant chalkboard in our church lobby now reads, "Our mission: to show you who Jesus is." Underneath, hundreds of handwritten definitions appear each week as people in our church celebrate who Jesus is to them.

Who Jesus Is to You

Take a minute, like the people in our church do, and think of some words that describe what you think of when you think of Jesus. What would you put on our bulletin board?

Jesus is _____

Jesus is _____

Jesus is _____

Jesus is _____

I can't think of a better mission in life. I'll probably write more books, but I doubt I will ever write one as important as this. At the same time, this book barely scratches the surface of who Jesus is. Discovering the depths of his love has become my passion and my delight.

The Bible

I am a Bible person. I don't believe my brain has been working long enough to figure out the meaning of life, and I need help. The Bible is an amazing, divine, supernatural book that shows us the plan of God. It gives us the right way of looking at life. I believe that God used humans to write it, but he guided what they wrote, and everything in it is true.

The Bible is meant to be down-to-earth. It was written for real people facing real issues. So when I preach and write, I often retell Bible stories in my own words. It's not a new version of the Bible; it's just the way I see it, usually with a few jokes thrown in. I think God laughs a lot more than we realize, by the way—after all, He's the one who invented humor in the first place.

Lame Bible Jokes

1. Why didn't Noah go fishing? He only had two worms.
2. Why didn't they play cards on Noah's ark? Noah was sitting on the deck.
3. What did Adam say the day before Christmas? Merry Christmas, Eve.

4. Who is the fastest person in the Bible? Adam. He was first in the human race.

5. Who was the biggest lawbreaker in the Bible? Moses. He broke all Ten Commandments at once.

My Sock-Drawer Brain

You'll find this out soon enough, so I might as well spell it out. I am not a very organized person.

That will make some of you happy and frustrate others. I have the attention span of a five-year-old.

Some people have brains like super-organized sock drawers, with all the socks folded and lined up in neat rows. Everything is organized and color-coded. If you are in charge of your life like that, that's awesome. God bless you.

But the drawers in my brain look like an explosion went off in them. Socks are everywhere, and some of them are mismatched and hanging off the lamp. So if I jump around a bit in this book, now you know why. It's just the way God made me, and although I almost drove my teachers and mom crazy growing up, I've learned to laugh about it now. And to apologize a lot to my wife.

A Final Note

I would not be who I am without my dad, Wendell Smith. He passed away from cancer in December 2010, and I miss him every day. He was my friend and my hero.

He and my mom, Gini, founded the City Church in 1992. They pastored for seventeen years before turning the church over to my wife, Chelsea, and me in 2009. My dad's faith, generosity, and love were one of a kind.

My father showed me who Jesus is. He started me on an amazing, exciting journey that's still going on.

My prayer is that as you read this book, you also would get to know Jesus for who he really is. And when you do, he will be better than you ever dreamed.

Jesus Is **YOUR FRIEND.**

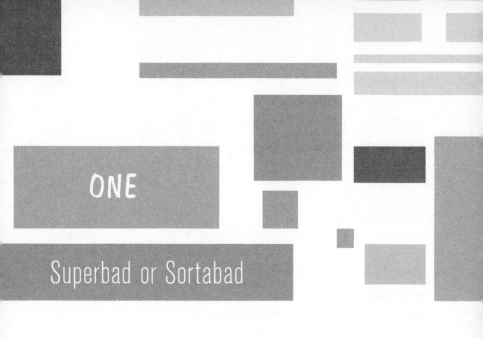

ONE

Superbad or Sortabad

"If God can help so-and-so, he can help *anyone!*"

I've heard myself say it a few times. "So-and-sos" are always real troublemakers, famous for being good at doing bad. They are awesome at sin, they sin a lot, and they enjoy their sin.

"Did you hear? Tyler got detention. That's, like, the third time this year! If God could get him straightened out, he could help anybody!"

"That girl calls herself a Christian, but can you believe what she did? She should be ashamed of herself. If God can help her, he can help anybody!"

Let's be honest. Mostly good people like to look down on mostly bad people. We enjoy feeling sorry for them, or even angry at them, acting like we are so much better. We love to hold them up as examples of just how bad people can get. Then we pat ourselves on the back and head off to make our grandmas proud.

Notice how I just included myself in the "mostly good" category. I didn't think about it. I just did it.

That's what bothers me the most.

The Badness Scale

The problem with saying "if God can save so-and-so then he can save anybody" is that it means we are rating sins and sinners on some badness scale that we made up.

Sin, by the way, is anything that goes against what God wants for us. God gives us certain instructions and rules for our own good, and if we step outside of those rules, we are sinning. We'll talk more about this later, but let me just say this right from the beginning: God is not nearly as mad about your sins and my sins as we think he is. Sure, he is concerned about them because he wants what's best for us, but he is not mad at us. He is madly in love with us. We'll talk about this in more detail later on.

Dictionary Entry

sin

noun

1: a breaking of a moral law

2: an action that is or is felt to be bad

synonym see OFFENSE

On our made-up badness scale, we label small sins, medium sins, large sins, extra-large sins, and supersized sins. If we see someone with small to medium sins, we think, *He's a pretty good person. He's nice and friendly to everyone. He's obviously close to Jesus. It won't be hard for God to forgive his sins.*

Then we see someone with medium to large sins, and we get more nervous. *We really have to pray for her. She is going downhill fast. God is going to have to get her attention the hard way. She really needs to work on fixing herself so she can get closer to God.*

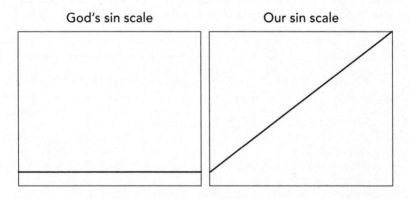

God's sin scale   Our sin scale

When we come across a supersize sinner, someone who commits the big sins, we just shake our heads in pity.

Nowhere in the Bible, though, do we find God labeling different levels of sin. God doesn't share our rating system. To him, all sin is equal, and all sinners are lovable—even the worst of us. Sure, sins have different consequences: some will get you thrown in jail or your face punched in, while others won't even be noticed. But God just calls sin, *sin*.

To GOD, all sin is equal, and all SINNERS are lovable.

Zacchaeus the Gangster

Jesus didn't have a rating system for sin either. He was willing to accept anyone, to love anyone. Nowhere is this more obvious than in the story of Zacchaeus the tax collector.

I should mention up front that when I read Bible stories, all the main characters have accents. That's just how my mind works. I've never been very good at concentration, so I suspect the accents are my brain trying to keep me focused.

Zacchaeus, in my mind, was a bit of a rapper. If you can't read his dialogue with some swagger, you and I are not going to connect very well for the next few pages.

In case you aren't familiar with the story, Zacchaeus was a tax collector. Actually, he was a chief tax collector. He was also really short. That's important.

Here's the story, straight from the Bible:

Jesus entered Jericho and made his way through the town. There was a man there named Zacchaeus. He was the chief tax collector in the region, and he had become very rich. He tried to get a look at Jesus, but he was too short to see over the crowd. So he ran ahead and climbed a sycamore-fig tree beside the road, for Jesus was going to pass that way.

When Jesus came by, he looked up at Zacchaeus and called him by name. "Zacchaeus!" he said. "Quick, come down! I must be a guest in your home today."

Zacchaeus quickly climbed down and took Jesus to his house in great excitement and joy. But the people were displeased. "He has gone to be the guest of a notorious sinner," they grumbled.

Meanwhile, Zacchaeus stood before the Lord and said, "I will give half my wealth to the poor, Lord, and if I have cheated people on their taxes, I will give them back four times as much!"

Jesus responded, "Salvation has come to this home today, for this man has shown himself to be a true son of Abraham. For the Son of Man came to seek and save those who are lost." (Luke 19:1–10)

Interesting backstory: Israelites of Jesus' day looked at tax collectors as thieves. Tax collectors were Jews who worked for the Roman government, which ruled Israel at the time. Their job was to collect taxes from their own people and hand the money over to the hated Romans. Their own income came from whatever they could get out of people after they collected the tax for Rome. So Zacchaeus and his fellow tax-collecting traitors would make up whatever amounts they wanted. Zacchaeus was a professional cheat. He took money from little old ladies. He was a thief.

I think Zacchaeus was probably up on pop culture, by the way. I think he liked making appearances; he liked being in on the action. When they rolled out the red carpet and the cameras showed up, Zacchaeus was going to be there, a lady on each arm, looking over his sunglasses at the TV crew. "Hey, y'all." He was tough. He was important. He was cool.

Zacchaeus was a short guy, but don't be deceived by his height. He had a lot of money. At some point, years before, he had been recruited by the Romans. He was probably a very smart guy. He would have started out as an assistant to a tax collector. After proving he was good enough, he would have been promoted to tax collector. Ultimately, when we find him in this story, he has become a chief tax collector. He probably oversees an entire tax district and a gang of mini tax collectors who give him a cut of their take.

This makes Zacchaeus a major reject. He is infamous, legendary, notorious. How long has he been doing this? Five years? Longer than that—he's a chief tax collector. Ten years? Twenty?

I don't think he minds being hated. In fact, I think he's loving life. He's up in his big house overlooking the city, lounging in his pool, with servants fanning him and dropping grapes in his mouth.

Everybody fears him now. Sure, they hate him—but at least they respect him. Back in elementary school, nobody picked the short guy. But now they're afraid of the little man. Zacchaeus is the big guy on the block.

Rumor was, Jesus might be the promised Messiah. Zacchaeus had grown up in the Jewish culture, and he would have been familiar with the prophecies. No doubt he had heard that one day there would come a Messiah. Now Jesus is coming through town, and Zacchaeus says, "I'm gonna check this guy out. He's getting a lot of followers; a lot of guys are talking about him. I'm curious."

I doubt Zacchaeus was thinking, *Man, I sure hope Jesus saves me.* Saves him from what? His big house? All the ladies who love him?

No, he just wanted to check out the popular guy. Zacchaeus was all about popularity and power. You don't become a tax collector and then a chief tax collector and not like money and fame. He was famous in a negative sense, but famous nonetheless.

Jesus starts strolling through. People are lining the streets, trying to catch a glimpse of him, and Zacchaeus realizes he can't see over the crowd. *This is messed up,* he says to himself. *I'm not gonna be able to see this dude.*

Zacchaeus is a guy who is used to getting his way. So he hitches up his robe, runs ahead, and climbs a little tree next to the road.

Sure enough, he can see the dust cloud and all the people clumped around Jesus. You'd think he was Justin Bieber or something. He's rolling down the street, and suddenly— Zacchaeus can't believe his luck—Jesus stops right next to the little man's tree.

This is sweet, he's thinking. *I can check this guy out from up here, maybe listen in on what he's got to say.*

Then, to Zacchaeus's surprise, Jesus looks up at him. He calls him by name. "Zacchaeus."

"Whaaaa? How do you know me? I don't know you. Who told you about me?"

They say the sweetest sound to a human being's ears is the sound of his or her own name. God calls this rejected, hardened, selfish man by his name: "Zacchaeus, hurry down! I'm heading over to your house—right now."

"You are? Uh, okay. Yeah."

Zacchaeus is loving life right about now. Everyone else, all the "good" people, want a minute with Jesus, a nod, a handshake. Yet now the chief tax collector—the biggest bad guy around—gets a personal invitation. I think he's looking at everyone saying, "Whassup now, y'all?" He sends word to all his cronies and tax collector minions to come over and meet this Jesus. This is his moment in the limelight.

"I'm Changing Everything"

But that afternoon, something unexpected and unexplainable began to happen in Zacchaeus's heart. How long did he spend time with Jesus, the living God? Two hours? Four hours? We don't know. What did they talk about? We can only guess.

We can assume that they ate a meal together and Jesus probably listened a lot. Zacchaeus must have thought, *Nobody listens to me, except for a few guys who work for me. But this guy cares. He listens. He gets it.*

I can imagine Zacchaeus looking into the kindest eyes he's ever seen and thinking, *Does Jesus know who I am? Does he know who is around my dinner table? Does he know what we do for a living? Does he know what paid for his fish? Does he know how I paid for this house? He must . . . but he doesn't reject me.*

After a few hours with Jesus, Zacchaeus can't contain himself any longer. Suddenly he stands up, overwhelmed with who this Jesus is. In front of family, friends, and employees, he blurts out, "I'm changing everything!"

What?

"I'm changing everything, Jesus. I'm gonna start giving my money away. In fact, anyone I've ever cheated, I'm gonna give them back four times what I stole."

The tough, money-hungry mob boss is about to go broke, and he doesn't even care. A moment with Jesus changed everything.

I wonder what Jesus said in one short afternoon that changed a lifelong taker into a generous giver. But that's not the point of this passage. I think the Bible skips over what they talked about because we'd try to turn it into a recipe or a program. It wasn't what Zacchaeus talked about—it was the person he talked about it with. It was about being with Jesus.

What changed Zacchaeus? Rules? Threats? Trying harder to be good? No—just a few moments with God in the flesh. We don't even have a record of anyone telling Zacchaeus he needed to repent or give the money back. But something came over this man when he encountered Jesus.

Hurry Down

The truth is, I am Zacchaeus. I'm not talking about how tall or short I am physically—I mean I'm "short" spiritually, in my own ability and my own potential. I don't measure up. I'm not good enough. Even if I want to get to Jesus, even if I want to see Jesus, I can't see past myself. I can't see past my sin, past my distractions, past my own pride.

> Something came OVER this man when he encountered JESUS.

You know how we usually try to reach Jesus? We run faster and we climb our little trees, like doing good things and praying and acting religious. We think, *I'll get to Jesus. I'll impress Jesus with who I am.*

I think a lot of people believe deep inside that they are not good enough, that they are too weak. No matter how hard they try or what they accomplish, they know they are not enough. There's nothing wrong with being short in a physical sense, but they are short in a spiritual sense. They have sinned and come short of God's standard. So they think, *I'll run faster,*

I'll run ahead, I'll find a tree and climb it, and I'll get God's attention.

As if your running and your climbing are what gets God's attention!

That's not what saved Zacchaeus. It was God's mercy. It was God's grace. It was God taking action.

We think God stops and takes notice of us because he sees us up in our cute sycamore trees. We think it is because we are so good. "See, I got God to notice. You see me? It's because I pray so loud, because I pray so much, because I go to church."

But that's not why Jesus stopped that day. He stopped of his own choosing. He stopped because he's gracious and he's good. He stopped because he knew Zacchaeus by name, just as he knows you and knows me.

> "I'm here to FIND and help lost PEOPLE. That's why I've come."

Jesus told Zacchaeus to hurry, and he tells us the same thing. "Hurry down from acting like you're perfect. Hurry down from traditions. Quit trying to pick yourself up. Only my grace can save you. Come down, and come now. Don't spend another moment or another day trusting yourself. I need to be with you today."

While Zacchaeus spoke, Jesus must have been smiling to himself. Now he makes an announcement of his own. "Today, salvation has come to this house. Zacchaeus is a son of Abraham, a true Jew."

Zacchaeus is stunned. He is the definition of a traitor, the bad guy, the opposite of a good Jew. For as long as he can remember, he's been on the outside looking in. Now he's on the inside? Now he's a good guy?

I wish I could have seen the look on his friends' faces. *If there's hope for Zacchaeus, there must be hope for me too!*

Then Jesus sums up his life mission: "I'm here to find and help lost people. That's why I've come."

The Pharisees, or religious leaders of the day, were expecting a Savior, a Messiah, sent from God to help their nation. They thought the Messiah was only coming for the chosen few, for the holy few, for the religious few. But Jesus said over and over that he came for the broken, the bad, the disappointing, the stuck, the deceived, the lost, the hurting.

Sometimes we are a lot like Zacchaeus. We've been at this sin thing ever since we were born. We have problems and weaknesses. We do wrong things. We've tried as hard as we can to change, but we still make so many mistakes. We wonder, *Why would Jesus even love me?*

Have you ever felt that way? Maybe it's a secret sin: something you're ashamed of that not even your best friend knows about. Maybe it's something that controls your life, like lying or being mean or some other thing you can't stop doing. By now you may be starting to believe that you'll never change.

> **JESUS** is not mad at you. He's not out to get you. He's **YOUR** friend and your **RESCUER.**

But Jesus is not mad at you. He's not out to get you. He's your friend and your rescuer. Like Zacchaeus, just spend time with Jesus. Don't hide from him in embarrassment or reject him in pride. Don't allow the opinions of other people to shape your idea of him. Get to know him for yourself, and let the goodness of God change you from the inside out.

Talk About It

1. Have you ever used a "badness scale" when thinking about yourself or someone you know? Why doesn't Jesus have a badness scale?

2. What are some ways people try to get ahead by "running and climbing" in life and impressing others, like Zaccheus did? How do you think they would act differently if they knew Jesus was already impressed with them?

3. When I say "spending time with Jesus," what does that mean to you? Since we can't have dinner with him like Zacchaeus did, what else can we do?

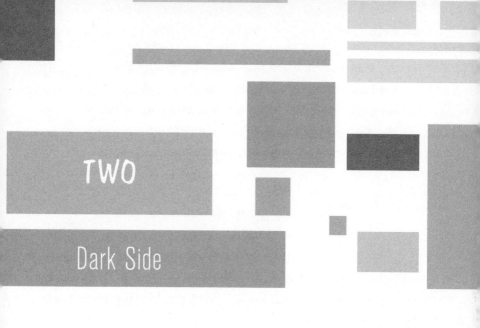

TWO

Dark Side

Zacchaeus wasn't the only tax collector to have his world rocked by Jesus. There was also Matthew. Matthew was one of Jesus' disciples, and the book he wrote, now part of the Bible, describes many key events in the three-plus years of Jesus' ministry.

Matthew's first encounter with Jesus shows that when it comes to sinners, God has two categories. Just two. Matthew 9:9–13 says,

> As Jesus was walking along, he saw a man named Matthew sitting at his tax collector's booth. "Follow me and be my disciple," Jesus said to him. So Matthew got up and followed him.
>
> Later, Matthew invited Jesus and his disciples to his home as dinner guests, along with many tax collectors and other disreputable sinners. But when the Pharisees saw this, they asked his disciples, "Why does your teacher eat with such scum?"

When Jesus heard this, he said, "Healthy people don't need a doctor—sick people do." Then he added, "Now go and learn the meaning of this Scripture: 'I want you to show mercy, not offer sacrifices.' For I have come to call not those who think they are righteous, but those who know they are sinners."

Two Kinds of Sinners

Like Zacchaeus, Matthew was a tax collector. Everywhere he went, he was hated, feared, and rejected. Until he met Jesus. Matthew never forgot how this man looked past his job and saw him as a person.

In Jesus' conversation with Matthew, he lumps all of humanity into two groups: people who *think* they are righteous and people who *know* they are sinners.

Group 1: Think They're Good	Group 2: Know They're Not
Have to compare themselves to others to see if they're okay.	Are happy with themselves because they know God loves and forgives them, even when they're not perfect.
Kind of enjoy judging other people when they mess up.	Know that sin is not okay, but have compassion for people even when they sin.
Make up their own "rules" to decide who is in or out, good or bad, cool or uncool.	Focus on the "Golden Rule": love your neighbor as you love yourself.

That's it. No sliding scale, no grading on the curve, no relative goodness. We either pretend we don't need him or we acknowledge we do.

One thing everyone has in common is that we all need help. The catch is that we don't all admit it. Rather than realizing everyone is in this together, that we are all in need of help, we often prop up our self-esteem by looking at people who do supposedly worse things than we do.

We need to abandon our "badness scale" and adopt God's way of thinking because our wrong labels keep us from the right kind of interaction with people. We assume we know where they are on the rating scale, and we assume we know whether they are ready to hear about Jesus and give their lives to God.

In reality, for many people, the biggest hurdle to receiving the grace of God is not their crazy sins—it's their empty good deeds. In other words, they think they are doing pretty good all by themselves, so they don't need Jesus' forgiveness and help.

It's obvious some people have problems. But for the kid who lives in a nice house with a nice family, dresses well, does his homework, walks his dog, gets along with other kids, respects his parents, and never cheats at school—for that model kid, it's not so obvious. He might compare his goodness to others' badness and think, *I'm a pretty good person. I'm doing better than most people. I don't need help.*

> One thing EVERYONE has in common is that we all NEED help. The catch is that we don't all ADMIT it.

Our superficial system for labeling "badness" also guarantees that we will never find freedom ourselves. It takes courage and humility to recognize we are as messed up as the worst people we know, and many of us never get that honest with ourselves. If we can't be honest with ourselves, we'll never be honest with God. We'll continue to cover up our dark sides and show off our good deeds, and nothing will ever change.

"Hi. I Hate You."

Jesus befriended sinners like Zacchaeus and Matthew, and the Pharisees especially couldn't handle that. Pharisees were the spiritual teachers of the day. They were experts in Jewish religious law—a set of hundreds of man-made rules that tried to apply the Ten Commandments to everyday life. They had regulations for everything from washing hands to tying loads onto camels.

When we find Pharisees in the Bible, they are usually doing one thing: pointing out sinners. Condemning people was part of their daily routine. They had made careers out of publically rejecting broken people. And because everyone has broken areas in their lives, they were never short of targets to point their fingers at.

The Pharisees loved keeping the law, but they didn't understand the love of God. They laid down judgment without mercy, punishment without love, criticism without understanding.

In the name of hating sin, the Pharisees ended up hating sinners.

Perhaps worst of all, they concluded that their separation from sinners was what made them holy. They tried to prove how good they were by pointing out how bad everyone else was.

That's why it was difficult for Jewish religious leaders to understand Jesus. They were waiting for a Messiah, a Savior, and they assumed he would be like them. He would wear fancy robes and be separate from nasty people. He would walk the streets with his head held high and expect everyone to get out of the way in fear. They assumed God would come and be just like them.

They were wrong.

Jesus made a point of seeking out sinners and befriending them. He wasn't concerned with his reputation. He wasn't trying to prop up his image by putting others down. He was God and he was perfect, yet he declared by his actions that he did not condemn even the worst sinners.

Ironically, Jesus' harshest words were directed at the Pharisees. He knew they were hypocrites. He saw through their fake spirituality. He called them out publicly, and they hated him for it. Ultimately, it was those religious leaders who demanded his crucifixion, and they stirred up the crowds until the Roman rulers were forced to carry out their wishes.

> JESUS made a point of SEEKING out sinners and befriending them.

Notorious sinners didn't kill Jesus. Phony religious people did.

The Pharisee in My Head

Before we get too furious at the Pharisees, though, realize that inside each of us is a Pharisee trying to get out. It's happened to me. No sooner do I conquer a bad habit than I become the biggest critic of anyone who still does what I just stopped doing.

Things the Pharisee in My Head Says to Me

- "Doesn't that guy realize how dorky he looks in those clothes? He'll never be as cool as you."
- "Don't let people see you talking to her—they might think you're friends, or worse, just as bad as she is."
- "Go ahead and make fun of that guy with your friends—it'll be fun. After all, he brought it on himself with all that stuff he does."
- "You're so much better than those girls over there. And it's because of your hard work and your intelligence. You deserve the credit for how good your life is."
- "Can you believe the bad things that guy does? What a terrible person. You should be glad you're not like him."

I find that righteous outrage comes a lot easier than humility and compassion. Mentally shaming other people for their bad deeds is more comfortable than dealing with my own.

We easily recognize when *other* people have problems. But think for a moment: those evil people most likely don't see themselves as evil. If they start to feel guilty, they just look a little further down the holiness food chain, find someone worse off, and start patting themselves on the back for not being that bad.

So now I have to ask myself, how come I assume I'm near the top of that food chain? And on a related note, who is looking at me and using my mistakes to prop up their self-esteem? Yikes. Just the thought makes me uncomfortable, but it's a fair question.

Here's what I often do. I make up rules that fit my life, then I judge you by them. If you follow my rules, you are a good person.

If you break my rules, you are a bad person. If you have stricter rules than I do, you're a stick-in-the-mud who needs to lighten up.

It's so convenient. And so wrong.

If our definition of *sin* is "doing bad things," then we can all agree that sin exists. People do bad things. Even if my definition of *bad* differs a bit from someone else's, we still agree that stealing is wrong. Murder is evil. Hurting people on purpose is awful.

The problem is that we don't like to think of ourselves as people who do these things. Other people sin. We just mess up.

But let's be honest. We aren't doing ourselves any favors by defining ourselves as good and others as bad. Let's just agree that we all need help, that we are all in this together. The good news is that Jesus came to reveal a God who measures us not by our actions but by his love.

Why, then, do I so easily start to judge when I look at people who seem "bad"? I can think of one reason, though I'd rather not admit it: my rules keep me at a distance from bad people.

If I separate myself from the people the world sees as bad, I don't have to deal with their pain. I don't have to walk in their shoes or love them or let my heart break with theirs. I don't have to get my hands dirty helping them or be kind to them when no one else will. I can justify rudeness and not caring when my heart should bleed with compassion. I can ignore the fact that it could have been me in their place.

If I separate myself from sinners, I don't risk my own reputation. I remain a member in good standing of the holier-than-you club, where we sit around congratulating each other on how much better we are than everyone else.

Scariest of all, if I separate myself from bad people, I feel better about myself. Because compared to them, I'm doing pretty well.

Again, please don't misunderstand. I don't think rules are horrible. It's how we use them that can be horrible. I have rules for my kids that are for their protection, and your parents and teachers have rules for the same reason. Our society has laws for our own good, and the Bible tells us to respect those in authority over us and to obey the law. I am completely in favor of authority, order, justice, and structure.

> **JESUS was obsessed with showing MERCY to those who least DESERVED it.**

We just have to remember that rules don't prove how spiritual we are or how close to God we are. If anything, they are proof of our sinfulness, a reminder that we all tend to do wrong and that we need help.

The Pharisees were so obsessed with obeying every bit of the law that they missed the point of the law: to love God and to love others. They thought their sacrifices made God happy while everyone else's sinfulness made him mad. Jesus showed them they couldn't be further from the truth. The sin of the people aroused God's compassion, not his anger. And the sacrifices of the self-righteous meant little to God because their hearts were actually far from him.

Jesus was obsessed with showing mercy to those who least deserved it. He was passionate about giving hope to hopeless people. He was committed to showing grace to the worst of sinners. And if I'm honest, that includes me.

I'm going to be honest with you: even though I'm a pastor, at times I still wrestle with wrong thoughts. I still get impatient with my kids. I still make decisions out of selfishness and evil rather than love. I'm sure you know what I mean—we all face this struggle. Whether I am better than you or worse than someone else really doesn't matter. What matters is that I recognize my need for Jesus.

Rather than rejecting people out of a false sense of holiness, rather than avoiding people who don't measure up to my standards, I need to remember that I am still desperately in need of Jesus' grace.

Jesus befriends the worst of sinners, so Jesus befriends me.

> Whether I AM better than you or WORSE than someone else really doesn't MATTER. What matters is that I recognize I need JESUS.

Talk About It

1. What are some "rules" about goodness and badness that you may have made up for yourself, like the Pharisees made up about hand washing or camel loading? Do they have to do with the way people look? Behave? What they say or do?

2. How do you behave toward people who aren't really considered "good kids"? How could you be more compassionate?

3. Have you noticed that some things that really annoy you about people are the same things that annoy you about yourself? Keep track of those annoying things this week and pray about them—both for the other person and yourself!

THREE

Real Life

I enjoy movies. That may be a shock to you because I'm a pastor, and you probably thought pastors only watch sermons and VeggieTales.

I will neither confirm nor deny whether I have actually seen the movie that I'm about to quote from. Let's just say I've heard from other people who saw it. They told me it's violent, and I'm not for violence. So like I said, I can neither confirm nor deny that I've seen this movie.

The movie is *Braveheart*. I've been told that in this movie, William Wallace makes a certain profound statement. So, of course, I did some research. I used some of my Internet resources, such as Wikipedia, and I discovered that we're not sure if William Wallace said this particular quote. But we certainly know Mel Gibson did.

"Every man dies, but not every man truly lives."

What a concept. It's worth thinking about.

That's the Life

Are you alive? You are breathing, you are functioning, your brain is more or less engaged, and you are reading this book. So yes, you are alive. Your parents even have official documents that prove your birth to anyone who might question it. You are sucking oxygen on planet Earth. You are alive.

But are you *really* living?

The apostle Paul described what it means to be truly alive in Ephesians 2:1–7:

> And you He made alive, who were dead in trespasses and sins, in which you once walked according to the course of this world, according to the prince of the power of the air, the spirit who now works in the sons of disobedience, among whom also we all once conducted ourselves in the lusts of our flesh, fulfilling the desires of the flesh and of the mind, and were by nature children of wrath, just as the others.
>
> But God, who is rich in mercy, because of His great love with which He loved us, even when we were dead in trespasses, made us alive together with Christ (by grace you have been saved), and raised us up together, and made us sit together in the heavenly places in Christ Jesus, that in the ages to come He might show the exceeding riches of His grace in His kindness toward us in Christ Jesus. (NKJV)

Many of us are always in hot pursuit of "the life." For example, we're stuck in traffic on a bridge, and we look down and see people waterskiing below and say, "Man, that's the life. That would really be living."

Or we turn on the TV and see some pop star showing off her crazy huge house. And we think, *She's really living the life. I want to be her. Then I could enjoy everything.*

But would living "the life" really satisfy us? To truly live, do we just need more money? Fame? A boat?

Those things are nice. Especially the boat. But in the pursuit of true life, they are just fake things—distractions. That's why many people go their whole lives without ever truly living.

Oh, sure, we all have our moments. This life will offer us good moments and laughter and joy and excitement and fun. But the truth is, at the end of the day, many of us lay our heads on our pillows and we know something's not right.

Cool gadgets can't make you truly alive. Upgrades to your cool gadgets can't make you truly alive. A stack of cash can't make you truly alive. Popularity can't make you truly alive. And your new headphones can't make you truly alive. They may look cool, but they can't bring life.

Missing the Mark

Let me go a step further. Is living in sin really living?

I suppose before we answer that question, we need to explain the reality of sin. If you have a brother or sister who is in the toddler stage, you already know sin is real. And it wears diapers. How can something so cute get so mad and so loud? In the mall? When your friends are watching? Obviously, no one has to teach us to be selfish, ungrateful, and angry. That's the factory default. We are born with a tendency to sin, which the Bible calls a sinful nature.

Lots of sincere people have tried to explain away sin, but the fact remains, there are evil people out there. All it takes is for someone to hit your mama and you know there is sin in the world. Even "good" people do a lot of evil things. Sin is all over the place. It's in me and it's in you.

God created Adam and Eve, the first man and the first woman, with a free will because he did not want a relationship with a bunch of robots. He wanted us to be able to make our own choices. He knew that forced love is not love at all. So God gave us the ability within ourselves to choose him or reject him.

FORCED love is NOT love at ALL.

Adam and Eve rejected God, and now throughout the ages, humans are born with a tendency to reject God and go their own way. That break from God's original plan is the root of all sin.

So right and wrong exist. I'm not one of those people who believe that what's right for you is right for you, and what's right for me is right for me. That breaks down pretty quickly when what's right for me hurts you. Suddenly you don't think it's right anymore. There are absolutes out there. Good people try to abide by them, and good governments enforce them.

Then there are areas that are neither right nor wrong, and we call them *amoral*.

Dictionary Entry

ā-'mȯr-əl

adjective

1. not being moral nor immoral

for example, a stone, a chair, or a stone chair may be considered *amoral*

Most of life is that way, actually. As long as we handle them properly, amoral areas can add to our joy and success. Money, for example, is amoral. Cars are amoral. Sports are amoral, except for maybe cricket—any game that takes five days to play must be sin. Apologies to my friends in England who play cricket for days on end. I'd rather finish the game sooner and get to the snacks.

There are also things that are wrong in certain cases, but not in others. In that sense, right and wrong can change. In Singapore, for instance, it's basically a crime to chew gum. But here in Seattle, we have a city landmark called the Gum Wall. It's down by Pike's Market, and people from all over the world, including probably Singapore, come and stick their nasty gum wad to a wall in an alley. It is the most disgusting thing you could imagine. But it's not sin. I wish it were, but it's not.

Things That Gross Me Out

1. Sharing a toothbrush with someone else.
2. Dog hair. Dog saliva. Dog . . . other stuff.
3. Watching people eat.
4. Shaking hands with someone who just licked his fingers.
5. Getting sneezed on from behind. Or from any angle, actually.
6. Having someone in front of you spit out of the car window. (It never works, people. Swallow it.)

The best definition I've heard for sin is "missing the target." There is a target: a goal, a standard, a mark. God established it. And we have all missed it.

There is nothing gray about it. Sin is sin. Wrong is wrong. No matter how we spin it, no matter what we call it, we have all sinned, and we continue to sin more often than we'd like to admit.

The first mention of sin in the Bible is in Genesis 4:7. Cain is angry with his brother, Abel, and God warns him not to give in to sin. "If you refuse to do what is right, then watch out! Sin is crouching at the door, eager to control you. But you must subdue it and be its master."

If you've heard the story, you know that Cain didn't subdue, or control, his sin. Not even close. He went out and killed his brother. It was the first murder in human history.

Ruling over sin is a nice idea, but the human race has never been very good at it. The Bible tells us time and time again that we are all sinners. Romans 3:23 says plainly, "For everyone has sinned; we all fall short of God's glorious standard."

Romans 3:10 says the same thing: "No one is righteous—not even one." To be righteous means you're in right standing with God. To be righteous means you can stand shoulder to shoulder with God because you are right and you are sinless and you are perfect. The Bible says there is not even one person like that.

We can try to be righteous. And I suppose we all do. We help an elderly lady cross the street, we open the door for somebody, we give five bucks to a homeless guy on the street corner. We do good things to try to fill the space inside that

> In all our **EFFORTS** to be good friends or sons or **DAUGHTERS** or brothers or sisters, something is still **WRONG**.

keeps telling us something's wrong. But in all our do-goodism, in all the hours we work on our homework, in all our efforts to be good friends or sons or daughters or brothers or sisters, something is still wrong.

The passage I quoted out of Ephesians says that we were dead in our sins. In other words, life under sin is not life at all. It's death. No matter how many afternoons we spend wakeboarding on the lake or how many gadgets and electronic devices we have in our room, if we are ruled by sin, we aren't alive. We're all card-carrying members of the walking dead. We have our moments, we do our best, but we're still not experiencing true life.

Can life in sin be called living? Not really. Sure, we're breathing. Sin will let us breathe for a while—but it will never let us truly live. That's how sin works.

So I've got good news and bad news. The bad news is, we are all sinners. The good news is, if you are a sinner, you fit right in with the rest of us.

No Ordinary Person

So where do we go? What do we do? Can we find a man or a woman we can nominate and vote into office who can solve the sin problem? Can we pass some powerful laws that will set humanity free from the sin problem? Is that our answer?

The problem with nominating one of our own is that person also has a sin problem. We can wink and look away and pretend everything is good, but the Bible clearly says we have all sinned. So the answer is not among us. The answer is not in one of our own. No regular person can help us.

The apostle Paul wrote the book of Ephesians in the Bible. Before he got to know God, Paul was not a good man. He thought he was a good man because he was a religious fanatic. In the name of religion, he barged into people's homes and dragged them off to jail because they didn't believe what he did. He was mean. He was an accomplice to murder. And he was pretty impressed with himself.

> Then GOD got a hold of his LIFE, and everything CHANGED

Then God got a hold of his life, and everything changed. He ended up writing nearly half the books of the New Testament.

Yet even after becoming one of the greatest spiritual leaders in the history of the church, he still lost the battle against sin from time to time (see Romans 7:24).

Jesus is the only man who has ever truly lived, because sin had no hold on him. It's sin that sucks the life out of our existence.

Jesus showed up on the planet overflowing with life because he knew no sin. Sure, he was tempted, but he resisted all temptation, and he lived for thirty-three years without sin.

Because he was the only person who ever truly lived, he is the only one who could solve the sin problem once and for all.

He made a way for us to really live.

Keep Swinging

The first few verses of Ephesians 2, which I talked about a few pages ago, paint a very sad picture of what life looks like apart from God and apart from Jesus. But then we get to verse 4.

"But God . . ."

I love it when God butts in.

And by the way, when God butted in right here, it wasn't because we e-mailed him. It wasn't because we called him. It wasn't because we sent someone out waving a white flag to tell God, "We're really sorry. We apologize for ignoring you. We'd like you to get involved with our lives again."

> JESUS made a way for us to really LIVE.

In fact, we liked ignoring him. We were enjoying missing the target. We were getting grins and giggles out of our sins.

"But God"—while we were still sinners, Christ died for us.

"But God"—he took the first step.

"But God"—he was driven by his own rich mercy and great love.

That's good stuff right there. God is "rich in mercy." He doesn't just have mercy—he has mercy with all kinds of layers. Mercy that knows no end. God is a God of second chances.

I know about second chances because my two boys played T-ball. Are you serious? The ball is stationary on a rubber T. How many swings do these kids get?

You watch a kid whiff it seven times, but then on the eighth swing, he brushes the bottom of the T, and the ball falls off. And the coach yells, "Run!"

That's a lot like God. We get one strike, then another strike, then another—and everybody is saying, "I can't believe this guy is still alive. I can't believe God is still blessing him."

> I love it when GOD butts in.

We keep swinging and swinging. And

God, who is rich in mercy, picks up the ball again. "Swing again, slugger. Just swing again."

Meanwhile, people watching us are shaking their heads. "He's out."

God says, "He's not out till I say he's out."

Ephesians 2 says that not only is God rich in mercy, he also has "great love." I like that phrase. Not just love—it's great love. I love a few people in this world, but my love is far from great. It's limited, and it falters, and it often has a selfish side to it.

> **GOD says, "He's NOT out till I say he's OUT."**

But God loves the world.

Who is this God with such layers of mercy and such amazing, great love? Who is this God who seeks out people who are dead and brings them to life, not because of their goodness or their potential but because he is full of mercy and love?

Some of us think God loves us because we have potential. *We look bad now,* we think, *but God saves us because we will amount to something someday.*

"Hey, Gabriel," we imagine God saying to his head angel. "Do you see that guy over there?"

"Uh, that walking disaster?"

"Yeah, that's the one. He's got potential."

"What? No way, God. You're wasting your time."

"No really—I can see it," we imagine God saying. "Once I work with him for a few years, he's going to be a good Christian. I think he can help me out."

That sounds spiritual. That sounds humble. But it's not. It's actually just another way of saying we deserved to be saved.

But we don't, because we all sin. Maybe we didn't do anything yet, but we flatter ourselves into thinking that God saved us because he knew what we could become.

Listen, God doesn't save us because we have potential. That's silly. We do have potential—that much is true—but God doesn't rescue us from the death of sin just so we can help him out. He doesn't need our help.

> He doesn't need our **HELP**. He just wants to **LOVE** us. He wants to be loved by **US**.

He just wants to love us. He wants to be loved by us.

God saw us, dead in our sins, and he couldn't sit still. His rich mercy and his great love propelled him to provide a way to bring us back to life.

That's why he sent Jesus.

In Jesus, every person can truly live.

Talk About It

1. When you think, *Ah, that's the life!* what do you think of? What makes it "the life" for you? How long can those things last?

2. What's something "amoral" (like money or ice cream or something else) that could change, depending on the situation, from good to bad? What makes it good or bad in those cases?

3. Think about sin being "missing the target," like an arrow missing the bull's-eye. When have you missed the target in school or at home? How did your teachers and parents react? How does God react when you miss the target?

FOUR

Friend of Sinners

Jesus went to Zacchaeus's house and became the guest of a notorious sinner. He went to Matthew's house and ate dinner with many tax collectors and other people with bad reputations.

In full view of everyone, he hung out with the worst of the worst. In that culture, to eat with someone was to identify with them. Jesus associated himself with people who were rejected by upstanding people. They were the butts of jokes and the targets of gossip. No self-respecting person would risk befriending them for fear that others would think they were just as bad.

By everyone's standards, Jesus was a good man. So making friends with bad people didn't make sense. Preaching at them, rebuking them, criticizing them, mocking them—that was expected. Even applauded. But sitting around a table telling jokes and enjoying life together? That was shocking. That was crazy.

But Jesus didn't care about the scandal. He cared about the scandalous.

He liked spending time with sinners. He was God and he was perfect, but he spent much of the three and a half years of his ministry hanging out with bad people. He talked with them, ate with them, cried with them, and served them. People weren't just charity projects to him. He cared about them and listened to them. He offered unconditional hope and compassion.

Don't misunderstand me here. I'm not talking about hanging out with bad people because you want to do bad things, or because they are cool, or because it's exciting. I'm talking about spending time with people others usually reject because you love them and want to help them. Remember, there might be times when your parents will ask you not to hang out with certain people because they are a bad influence or they are making dangerous decisions. If that is the case, you need to trust that they know what they are doing.

"Healthy people don't need a doctor," Jesus said. "Sick people do" (Mark 2:17). That's why he spent his time with the needy, the helpless, and the lost. He came down to their level because they could never rise to his. He wasn't out to prove how good he was or how bad they were. He just wanted to offer them hope.

> You DON'T have to be GOOD to be Jesus' FRIEND. You just have to be HONEST.

Jesus isn't just a friend of sinners; he is *only* the friend of sinners. In other words, Jesus is the friend of people who are willing to admit that they have problems. If we understand that we have issues, if we recognize that we have stuff we cannot fix by ourselves, then Jesus is near to us.

You don't have to be good to be Jesus' friend. You just have to be honest.

Where Are Your Accusers?

We have to understand something about God: he isn't intimidated by sin the way we are. Usually when people tell us about something they did wrong, we're like, "You did what? With who? That's insane. And then what? How? Man, you're going to be in trouble!"

There is a story in John 8 where a pack of religious people dragged a woman before Jesus. They told him and the crowd around him that she had been caught in a sin that deserved the death penalty. Then they asked Jesus what should be done with her. They expected him to throw down judgment on her. After all, religious law demanded that she be stoned to death for such a sin.

But Jesus didn't throw any stones. He didn't gasp in holy horror. He didn't blush or look away. Instead, he looked past her sin and saw *her*, and his heart was moved with compassion. Then he turned to her accusers. "Let the one who has never sinned throw the first stone."

Well, when you put it that way . . .

The woman's accusers, ashamed, slipped away one by one, beginning with the oldest. It's funny, the older you get, the more you realize how dumb it is to be proud. These people realized they weren't exactly angels themselves, and they sneaked away.

Jesus looked back at the woman. "Where are your accusers? Didn't even one of them condemn you?"

"No, Lord," she replied.

And Jesus said, "Neither do I. Go and sin no more."

I've been in church a long time, so I'm sure I've read that story dozens of times. But lately, it's actually starting to sink in. Maybe it's because, like that woman's accusers, I'm a little older now, and I'm aware that I'm not such a good person after all. I can imagine myself in her place: trapped by a bunch of bad decisions, terribly alone, defenseless before a crowd of shouting judges who hold my life in their hands. And then, when hope is lost, the one who truly has the right to condemn me looks at me. In his eyes I read something completely unexpected.

Compassion.

Understanding.

Hope.

> The ENEMY is not bad people—it's BADNESS itself.

We are often harsher judges than God himself. The evil in others arouses our righteous anger, so we put on our judges' robes and pound our gavels without ever taking time to hear their stories. We condemn people to life sentences without parole, while God in heaven is saying, "Wait! I love that guy. There is hope for that girl. They can be saved."

The fact that Jesus is a friend of sinners is good news for me. Maybe my sins aren't as obvious as those of the woman in this story, but they are just as real. And had I been born into a different situation, I cringe to think who I would be, what I would have done, whom I would have hurt.

The enemy is not bad people—it's badness itself. And since we all have a measure of badness, who are we to cast the first stone? When it comes to sin, the only one who has a right to condemn others is Jesus. And he refused.

On this journey to understand Jesus, here are the stages I went through. Each one represents an *Aha!* moment (or an *Oh, shoot!* moment), where I realized I was living on false ideas of good and evil.

> Stage 1. I am a good person, and it is okay for me to criticize bad people.
>
> Stage 2. I am a good person, but I should show compassion to bad people.
>
> Stage 3. I am a sinner who needs just as much help as the next guy.
>
> Stage 4. I am loved by Jesus, just as I am, and so is everyone else.

I have to keep reminding myself to live in stage four, because I tend to circle back to stage one without even noticing.

If Jesus could say just one thing to you right now, what would it be? In my experience, most people would expect him to tell you something you're doing wrong. We think that if Jesus had only one shot at fixing us, he'd make it count by pointing out where we were blowing it the worst.

"You've got to stop losing your temper with your parents."

"Come on, try harder. Work harder. Be strong. Stop whining."

"You gossiped again? What were you thinking? Get your life together—or else!"

> JESUS isn't yelling at us to CLEAN ourselves up so we can be WORTHY of him. He loves us right now, just as WE are.

No, I think if Jesus had one shot at fixing us, he'd tell us how much he loves us. That's what Zacchaeus experienced. And Matthew. And the woman caught in sin. And countless other imperfect people.

Jesus loves us right now, just as we are. He isn't standing over us, yelling at us to clean ourselves up so we can be worthy of him. He is wading waist-deep into our troubles, weeping with us when we cry, rescuing us when we're lost, and healing us when we're sick.

Don't get me wrong—of course sin is bad. Sin hurts us and it hurts others. But the Bible is clear: we are going to sin. Sooner or later, willpower and education and good manners just won't be enough. We'll mess up. So if our hope is in just "being a good person," we are—to put it scientifically—toast.

Jesus sees our sin more clearly than anyone, yet he loves us more than anyone. He's not going to write us off, no matter what we've done. Yes, he's grieved by the sin. Sin hurts us, and he hates that. But our badness does not change for an instant the awesome love God has for us. If anything, it makes him that much more determined to rescue us. He will never give up on us, no matter how much we run from him.

Nobody is beyond hope. No sin is so great that Jesus cannot cover it. His love is so deep and wide that he can, in one moment of our faith, forgive our past, present, and future sins. Sin is simply not a problem for God.

As a pastor, I don't want people in my church to think they have to hide their sins and their sadness when they come on Sunday. If sinners aren't welcome at my church, then I'd better find a new church—because I'm a sinner too. And I'm the worst of all, since I know better.

Church is a place where a bunch of people who realize they need help get together to love Jesus and encourage each other. And then something happens: we start to change. God transforms us one area at a time. We hardly know how it happens, but one day we look around and realize that we're getting along with our family. We like the people we're around, and they like us back. We talk nicer to people and we get mad less often. And we can't take the credit for the change, because we just fell in love with Jesus. God did the hard part.

Jesus told the woman accused of sin to "go and sin no more." That wasn't a threat. It was a statement of freedom. He wasn't interested in making her feel bad for her past. He wanted to rescue her future. Jesus knew she didn't want to sin. Who starts out with the goal of being a bad person? But hard situations and wrong choices can trap us, and we can feel hopeless. Jesus came to break the cycle of sin and guilt and to give us back our future.

> **CHURCH** is a place where a bunch of **PEOPLE** who realize they need help get **TOGETHER** to love Jesus and **ENCOURAGE** each other.

The Smith Family Motto

Every day when I drop my kids off at school, I say the same thing: "Kids, remember, we are Smiths. What does that mean?"

Then together we repeat this mantra, "We are kind and encouraging, and we look for lonely people."

Dictionary Entry

mot-to

noun

1 : a phrase that describes the beliefs or values that are important to a person, family, or organization

---

My oldest son, Zion, rolls his eyes sometimes, as if to say, *Dad, just hurry, I'm going to be late.* He gets that from his mom; being on time doesn't rate high on my value scale. But people do. They are at the very top, and I want to teach that to my kids throughout their lives.

There are no shortcuts to real friendship with someone. Sometimes friendships are messy. Sometimes they are hard work. But our friends need us to show them the love of Jesus— even when they are having a bad day, even when they make mistakes, and even when they hurt our feelings.

God shows us what real love is in John 3:16, probably the most famous verse in the Bible. "For God so loved the world that He gave His only begotten Son, that whoever believes in Him should not perish but have everlasting life" (NKJV).

> Friends have to KNOW we like them in both the GOOD times and the BAD.

God so loved the world. He loved the whole world; not just the good part of the world, the part that loved him already, or the part that he knew would love him back. We need to expand our hearts, our comfort zones, and our friend zones.

He gave his only Son. He was willing to

make real sacrifices to build real relationships. Sometimes we need to put aside things and activities for the sake of people. Like Jesus, we need to be open to the people around us.

Whoever. He showed unconditional love and acceptance—for everyone. Love is risky. We might be rejected. We might be criticized and hurt by the people we are trying to help. But ultimately, love will win.

Ways to Expand Your Friend Zone

- Believe everyone likes you unless they tell you otherwise. That's what my dad used to say, and it works!
- Look at people in the eyes. Oh, and smile. Otherwise it's a little creepy.
- Compliment people. "I love your socks."
- Pray for someone without them knowing it, especially someone who is mean to you. You'll be amazed at what happens.
- Make our motto your own: be kind and encouraging, and look for lonely people.
- Don't be a critical person. Give people a chance. It's funny how often people you don't like at first end up being great friends later on.

My church is in the city of Seattle. It's my hope that we can show the people here how God sees them—that he loves them, no matter what—and show them what Jesus was like.

Growing up in church, I somehow got this weird idea that most people think sin is fun and God is boring. But really, most of the people in our city would like to know the Jesus we know. Maybe all they've seen in their lives is a Jesus who glares down from the ceilings of cathedrals or hangs in a picture on the wall. They've heard he was a good man, a good religious teacher, but do they know he is a friend of sinners? Do they know he's not mad at them? That he experienced life on earth and understands what they are going through? Do they know he is here to help?

Have you ever asked someone, "Hey, can I pray for you?" More often than not, even the people in my city—where not very many people go to church—will accept prayer gratefully.

Most of them have figured out long ago that being bad is overrated. They wish they could do better, that they could be less selfish, that they could overcome temptation, that they could control their tempers.

Does that struggle sound familiar? It should. Can you relate? I bet you can. Because whether we are "good" people or "bad" people, whether we have known Jesus for years or are just thinking about him for the first time—we all need Jesus. We are all seated at a table, surrounded by other sinners, listening to Jesus.

Jesus is the friend of sinners, so Jesus is our friend.

Talk About It

1. The Smith family motto is "We are kind and encouraging, and we look for lonely people." If you had to make a motto to encourage you or your family to do the right thing, what would it be? Write down a few examples in the blanks

below, and maybe even sit down with your parents or siblings this week and see what they think.

   a.

   b.

   c.

2. How can you tell when people are lonely? How can you be kind to them? Have you ever been lonely and had someone be nice to you? Tell about that time.

3. Think of a person you know who might be going through a tough time. How would you pray for him or her? If you have a chance this week, tell the person you are praying, or ask if you can pray with him or her. You'll be surprised how much that means to people!

Jesus Is GRACE.

FIVE

Embrace Grace

I'm a hugger. I like to hug. Growing up, I was taught "hugs, not drugs." But I've noticed that some people are not good huggers. It's not their fault—they obviously never learned how to hug back. You try to give them a warm bear hug, and they turn sideways and bounce you off their hip. Or they hug on the same side you do and you almost kiss. Or they get all tense and rigid, and you feel like you are hugging a mannequin with a robotic arm. Those are awkward hugs.

I remember when I was at a resort with my wife, Chelsea, and we were trying to get into the place where we were staying, but we didn't have keys. It was late at night, probably twelve thirty or so. So this older gentleman came out and opened the door for us. Nice man—he had been asleep, I'm sure, and he came out in his pajamas and let us in. Chelsea wanted to thank him, so she went to give him a hug, and all of a sudden he twitched and jerked like he was having some sort of fit.

Typical guy. No idea what to do with a hug.

That's how we often react when God's grace comes at us. It's awkward. God offers us something that's too good to be true—unearned, total forgiveness—and we stand there, stiff and uncomfortable, waiting for the hug to stop so we can get back to the business of earning our way into heaven.

We need to accept grace. We need to learn how to hug back.

How to Greet Around the World

- Rubbing noses (the Maori tribe of New Zealand)
- Sticking out your tongue (Tibet)
- Pressing your nose and top lip against the other person's skin and breathing on them (Greenland)
- Bowing (Japan, China, and more)
- Pressing your face against the other person's check and sniffing (Tuvalu island, Polynesia)
- Kissing each other on the cheek (many nations)
- Handshake, then a kiss on the nose (Oman)
- Slow handclap (Shona people of Zimbabwe)

What Is Grace?

Grace is hard for most people to define, let alone accept. The word is found throughout the Bible. In fact, it is pretty much the most important concept and word in the Bible. Grace is the foundation of Christianity and the basis of salvation. So we should probably understand it.

Webster's has eight different definitions for grace, including these four that you have probably heard before:

- A charming or attractive trait or characteristic ("carry yourself with grace")
- Approval, favor ("remain in his good graces")
- A title of address ("Your Grace")
- A short prayer at a meal ("Say grace over dinner")

Webster's top definition, however, comes closest to the biblical meaning of grace: "Unmerited divine assistance given humans for their regeneration or sanctification."

If you're like me, your eyes glazed over a bit when you read that. I'm sure someone smarter than I am was blessed just by reading it, but I need an example, a real-life story, for it to make sense to me.

One thing I love about Jesus is that he spoke in simple terms. He didn't talk forever and use big words in order to impress people. He told stories. If he were on earth today, everyone would follow him on Twitter and read his blog because he was real. He was authentic. What he said made sense. It went straight to the heart of the matter.

My favorite story Jesus ever told is what we call the parable of the prodigal son, which is found in Luke 15. *Parable* is a fancy word for a made-up story with a moral, like Aesop's fables ("The Tortoise and the Hare," and other such stories). *Prodigal* means "wasteful," but the story of the prodigal son has become so well known that the term can describe anyone who skips out on an area of life and then returns.

A parable is meant to teach something, so in order to understand this one, we have to understand the world and culture Jesus was telling the story in. In this case, religious people are once again criticizing Jesus because he was a friend of sinners. Luke 15 states, "Tax collectors and other notorious sinners often came to listen to Jesus teach. This made the Pharisees and teachers of religious law complain that he was associating with such sinful people—even eating with them! So Jesus told them this story . . ."

> **Jesus was AUTHENTIC. What he said made SENSE.**

Actually, Jesus told three in a row. All three parables answered the complaints of these religious individuals who said, at least in my brain, "Why in the world would you go to Red Robin and have Cajun Clucks and fries with those shady critters?"

The first story is about a lost sheep. Jesus described a shepherd who leaves the rest of the flock in the safety of the fenced-in field and goes into the wilderness to find a lost sheep. When he finds it, he throws a party to celebrate. Then Jesus gave the moral of the story: "In the same way, there is more joy in heaven over one lost sinner who repents and returns to God than over ninety-nine others who are righteous and haven't strayed away!"

Party Games in Heaven

1. Pin the Wings on the Angel
2. Halo Ring Toss
3. Tag (but you get to *fly*)
4. Piñatas with gold, silver, and diamonds inside

5. Hide-and-Seek (but you get to walk through walls, disappear, walk on water, and all kinds of cool stuff)

The second story is about a lost coin. Again, Jesus described a desperate search for something lost and the major celebration that follows when it is found. He finished with, "In the same way, there is joy in the presence of God's angels when even one sinner repents."

Side note: when "bad" people turn their lives around—in other words, when they *repent*—all of us who are "good" should echo the celebration that is happening in heaven. That's why I think we should smile in church—we should dance, we should celebrate, we should laugh, and we should get over our serious selves and represent the joy of heaven.

> We should SMILE in church—we should DANCE, we should celebrate, we should LAUGH, and we should get over our serious selves and represent the JOY of heaven.

Another side note: I've heard people say that religion is boring, living in purity is lame, and they'd rather be partying with their friends. Sorry, but that's messed up. If anyone knows how to throw an over-the-top, blow-your-mind kind of party, it's the Creator of the universe, the one who invented fun and pleasure. I'm just saying.

Ways to Show Joy in Church

1. Say hello to people; shake hands; give hugs. The goal is to make them feel special.

2. Sing as loud as you want! God doesn't care if you sound like One Direction or more like Shrek.
3. Offer to volunteer, and then help with a smile on your face.
4. Look for people you don't know very well and make new friends.
5. Take a selfie having fun with your friends, and tag your church when you post it.

The final story, the parable of the prodigal son, is the longest of the three, but it's worth reading even if you have heard it before.

"A man had two sons. The younger son told his father, 'I want my share of your estate now before you die.' So his father agreed to divide his wealth between his sons.

A few days later this younger son packed all his belongings and moved to a distant land, and there he wasted all his money in wild living. About the time his money ran out, a great famine swept over the land, and he began to starve. He persuaded a local farmer to hire him, and the man sent him into his fields to feed the pigs. The young man became so hungry that even the pods he was feeding the pigs looked good to him. But no one gave him anything.

When he finally came to his senses, he said to himself, "At home even the hired servants have food enough to spare, and here I am dying of hunger! I will go home to my father and say, 'Father, I have sinned against both heaven and you, and I am no longer worthy of being called your son. Please take me on as a hired servant.'"

So he returned home to his father. And while he was still a long way off, his father saw him coming. Filled with love and compassion, he ran to his son, embraced him, and kissed him. His son said to him, "Father, I have sinned against both heaven and you, and I am no longer worthy of being called your son."

But his father said to the servants, "Quick! Bring the finest robe in the house and put it on him. Get a ring for his finger and sandals for his feet. And kill the calf we have been fattening. We must celebrate with a feast, for this son of mine was dead and has now returned to life. He was lost, but now he is found." So the party began.

Meanwhile, the older son was in the fields working. When he returned home, he heard music and dancing in the house, and he asked one of the servants what was going on. "Your brother is back," he was told, "and your father has killed the fattened calf. We are celebrating because of his safe return."

The older brother was angry and wouldn't go in. His father came out and begged him, but he replied, "All these years I've slaved for you and never once refused to do a single thing you told me to. And in all that time you never gave me even one young goat for a feast with my friends. Yet when this son of yours comes back after squandering your money on prostitutes, you celebrate by killing the fattened calf!"

His father said to him, "Look, dear son, you have always stayed by me, and everything I have is yours. We had to celebrate this happy day. For your brother was dead and has come back to life! He was lost, but now he is found!" (Luke 15:11-32)

Three stories. Three lost things. Three parties. Jesus really, really wanted these self-righteous people to understand something: God loves bad people and rejoices when they turn to him.

The Pharisees couldn't believe that God would actually celebrate sinners. Yell at them? Yes. Make them pay for their evil? Without a doubt. But throw a party? What? They couldn't wrap their religious, rule-focused minds around that level of grace. They couldn't hug grace back.

What did the SHEEP do to be found? He didn't do a THING.

I've heard the story of the prodigal son preached dozens of times. For that matter, I've preached it myself more than once. We preachers usually focus on how dumb the son was and how terrible sin is. But this story is more about the father than about the son. It's more about love than about sin. The son wasted his money with crazy, over-the-top living. The father restored his son with crazy, over-the-top grace.

Look back at the first two stories. What did the sheep do to be found? He didn't do a thing. If anything, he probably ran farther away. Sheep are dumb like that. Or so I've been told—I've never herded sheep, and it's safe to bet I never will. And what about the coin? What did it do? Nothing. It just hung out with dust bunnies in the corner until the woman found it.

We don't preach sermons about how sorry the sheep was or about how desperately the coin sought out its owner. But when it comes to the story of the prodigal son, we like to focus on how sorry he was, as if that somehow earned him forgiveness.

It didn't. In everyone's minds, he had blown not only his reputation and his inheritance but also his right to be treated like the man's son. He had rejected his father publicly. When he sloshed through the pigsty mud, he dragged the family name behind him.

Yes, his repentance was important, because without it he wouldn't have returned to the father. But no amount of being sorry or embarrassed could ever make him worthy of being accepted. That was a gift, given for free.

Dear Dad

I have an issue with the little speech the son prepared, actually. I can imagine him trying to write it. He has just decided to go back and become a servant in his dad's house because his dad was so good that even the servants always had enough to eat.

But a thought stops him. *I can't just go back with nothing. I've got to have something to say to convince him to take me back.* So he sits down, grabs a scroll, dips a feather in ink, and starts to write a speech.

"Dear Dad, you're the greatest! Sure missed you . . ." *No, that's stupid.* He crumples it up, dips the feather in ink again, and starts to write.

"Dearest Father, if I lined up all the fathers in the world and had to pick one, I would pick . . ." *No, that's stupid too.* Throws it out.

"Hey, Dad, sure miss playing catch with you in the back . . ." *No, that's not it either. Just get to the point.*

> No amount of being **SORRY** or embarrassed could ever make him **WORTHY** of being accepted. That was a **GIFT**, given for free.

"Dear Dad, I've sinned against heaven, against you, against everyone, and I'm no longer worthy to be your son. Just make me one of your servants." He folds up the speech, finds a motorcycle, and gets some goggles and a map before heading back to his dad's house.

But wait. Here's my problem with that speech. What does he mean, "I'm no longer worthy"? When was he *ever* worthy?

I have three kids, all in kindergarten or elementary school. What if one of them came to me one evening and said, "Dad, I think I've finally done it. I've been super good lately, and I think maybe, just maybe, I'm worthy to be your child"?

I think I'd be a bit ticked, actually. I'd be like, "Worthy? Kid, you don't know what you're talking about." They are my kids. I love them. I would die for them. I'd do anything for them. It's never been about how good or bad they are, and it never will be. Being a son or daughter has nothing to do with being worthy— just ask your parents. We are sons and daughters of God by birth, not by worth. That's why Jesus says we must be born again.

No baby is born as a result of his or her own efforts. The doctor doesn't holler at a mom's tummy with a megaphone, "Come on, kid, try harder! Work harder! Bust out of there! It all depends on you!" The mom works hard, but the baby is just along for the ride.

Spiritual birth happens by grace when we believe. Ephesians 2:8–9 says, "For by grace you have been saved through faith, and that not of yourselves; it is the gift of God, not of works, lest anyone should boast" (NKJV).

Believe what? Simply that Jesus exists, that he paid for our sins when he died, and that he rose again to make new life available for each of us. Being a child of God is not based on what we do or what we are supposed to do, but on what Jesus already did. Our faith is in him, not in ourselves.

Why Did Jesus Have to Die?

- First, God loves you. He would do anything for you.
- You have sinned, just like everyone else. Sin kills, and sin separates us from God, who is perfect in every way.
- God can't just ignore sin, because that would be unfair, and God can't be unfair.
- God's solution: Jesus.
- Jesus is God, but he became a human. He never sinned, so he is the only person who didn't deserve to die.
- But Jesus died the death we deserved. He took all our sins on himself, and he paid the price for them once and for all. All we have to do is believe that this is true.
- Now we don't have to worry about death. Yes, our bodies will die someday, but we will live forever with God because Jesus took away all our sins.

Some of us knew that we were saved by grace a long time ago, but somehow, somewhere, we got off track. We started to think, *Now that we are Christians, now that we know better, we have to do something to keep up our standing with God.* We have to strive and stress and strain to stay on the straight and narrow.

What? Where did we get that? Jesus died for us before we were born, before we had done anything, good or bad. Why would he make us live by rules and law now?

Grace Runs Toward You

Back to our story. The boy is not even home yet when his father spots him in the distance. The man must have been out on his porch every night for months, maybe even years, making a fool of himself in front of the neighbors, scanning the horizon, hoping against hope to see a familiar figure coming down the lane.

"Give it up, man," his neighbors and friends must have said. "Your son hates you. He's lost to you. He's a failure. Stop wasting your time waiting for him. That boy doesn't deserve your love."

But the father never gave up. To him, it had nothing to do with what was deserved, what was fair, or what was expected. It wasn't about following rules. It was about his son. This was personal.

The Bible says, "While he was still a long way off, his father saw him coming." So the son is coming. He's trying his hardest. He's on his little motorcycle. *I'm going to find Dad.* He's looking at the map, thinking, *I haven't been this far away from home before. How do I get back to Dad's house again?* He's trying in his own strength.

> Being a child of GOD is not based on what we DO or what we are supposed to do, but on what JESUS already did.

And then all of a sudden he sees this man in a long robe and flip-flops running at him.

It's Dad.

We think, *Wow, that's nice, the father ran.* I've heard that in the Middle Eastern culture of the day, men didn't run. It was undignified for a man to run, especially for someone as wealthy and important as this boy's dad.

Remember, while Jesus is telling this story, there is a crowd of regular people gathered around him. They are wondering why Jesus goes to Starbucks and has a double vanilla extra hot latte with Mr. Tax Collector. So Jesus explains that this boy was trying to find his dad, and he was still a long way away. In other words, he was a long way away from being "righteous"—just like the bad people everyone was upset about. And the father *ran* to him.

When Jesus said "ran," I guarantee that everyone sucked air, because they were thinking, *I never saw my daddy run. Dads don't run.*

What was Jesus trying to say?

Crazy love. Super, over-the-top, overflowing love. Love that filled up the father so much that he didn't care about what the neighbors thought or what other people were saying. He just wanted to hug his son again.

I remember being at soccer practice with my son Zion when he was four. I was on the sideline with Eliott, who was two. Zion started his little scrimmage, which was kind of a disaster. It was a cute disaster though. There was a bunch of four-year-olds running around like they had no idea what they were supposed to be doing. Then all of a sudden the ball jumped out of the pack and bounced toward the goal. Zion broke away from the team in hot pursuit. I jumped to my feet, screaming, "Go, son! Go!" And I started running down the sideline. "Kick the ball in the goal!"

I should mention that there were no other parents at soccer practice. This was basically a substitute for daycare. I'm sure the coach was thinking, *Dear Lord, who is this man?*

Zion was a four-year-old, but you would have thought it was the World Cup of preschoolers, and I was knocking over imaginary cameramen and Gatorade tables as I ran next to my kid. "Kick the goal, son!" The whole time I was making big sweeping motions with my foot, just in case he didn't know what I meant.

At this point Zion was looking at me—he wasn't even looking at the ball—and he was smiling, basking in my pride. Then he accidentally swiped his foot, and the ball bounced off his ankle and dribbled into the goal.

"Yeeeeeaaaahh! Yes! Yes! Wow! That's my boy. Yes!" I screamed shamelessly. I pulled off my shirt and waved it around my head. Then I picked Zion up and paraded him around the soccer arena on my shoulders.

> It's CRAZY love. It's a father's LOVE.

Afterward, sanity returned and I realized what I had just done. The nice college guy who was coaching my four-year-old was looking at me, and he was thinking, *You need attention. You need help.*

Growing up, I had watched other dads overreact at games. I always swore I wouldn't do that, and here I was at practice—not even a real game, for crying out loud—and I had lost my mind. But when they are your own kids, you forget your manners. I can't explain it. I didn't plan it. I didn't think, *Today I will cheer for my son.* I just got caught up in the moment.

It's crazy love. It's a father's love.

In this parable of the prodigal son, the father represents our heavenly Father—God. He celebrates every little thing we do. He's constantly posting photos of me on a heavenly version of Instagram, and the angels are like, "God, what's the big deal? The guy is a dork."

And God says, "Yeah, he's a funny kid. But he'll grow out of that, and it doesn't matter because I'm so proud of him."

Even in our worst moments of selfishness, God still loves us. No matter what. And the moment he sees a hint of repentance, he goes crazy. He wraps us up in a huge bear hug. He calls for the robe, the ring, the sandals. He throws a party in our honor.

That is grace.

Too Good to Be True

I'm getting ahead of the story. The prodigal son deserved to be punished. Disowned. Banished from his father's presence forever. He knew it, and so did the crowd of people listening to Jesus. But now, before he can walk to his father, his father runs to him. Luke wrote, "Filled with love and compassion, he ran to his son, embraced him, and kissed him." One translation of the Bible says his father "fell on his neck" (Luke 15:20 KJV). It's a bear hug. He smothers him. He ignores what's considered proper, and he covers him with kisses.

The boy is tired, lonely, filthy, broken by what's happened to him. He stinks. He barely made it home. Now everything in him wants to fall into his father's arms, to be a little boy again with no cares or fears.

But buried in his father's arms, he remembers something. He doesn't deserve this. This isn't right. This isn't fair. That's what logic says, anyway. He tries to wiggle his way out of the hug so he can give his speech.

You have to understand that the people listening to Jesus' story have been living under strict, unforgiving laws their whole lives. They think exactly the way the boy is thinking. Right about now, though, they are wondering, *Who is this Jesus? How can he speak of such love? The Pharisees and the priests say that you get what you deserve. That you've got to do everything right. That you've got to pray and read the Bible. You have to know all the right words and be perfect. But this man is speaking of a kind of love I've never heard of before.*

When Jesus talks about the speech the boy had prepared, I guarantee everyone listening is thinking to themselves, *Now that's a good speech. That speech is going to work. You watch, he's going to win over his dad with that one.* They're thinking, *Oh, I'll take notes on that speech. I like that.* They didn't get it.

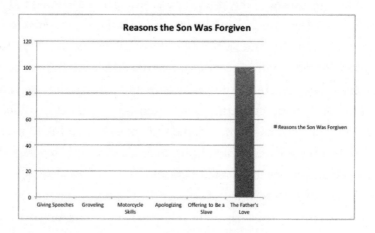

The son squirms free and launches into his plea: "Uh, Dad, I've sinned against you, and I'm no longer worthy—"

Midspeech, his dad stops him. He ignores his performance. It doesn't matter anyway, because the father has already forgiven the boy. He calls for servants to bring new clothes and a ring to put on the boy. He announces a massive party in honor of his son.

Honor? What did the son do to deserve honor? That was the question the boy's older brother asked. It was the question the Pharisees and the rest of the crowd were asking. And more likely than not, it's the question you and I ask every time grace runs at us.

He didn't *do* anything. It wasn't about him. It was about the grace of the father. The son simply had to accept the forgiveness the father offered him.

Confused but suddenly hopeful, the son enters his father's house. The party starts. People are overjoyed to see him. They welcome him home. There is no shame, no guilt, no rejection.

> He didn't DO anything. It wasn't about HIM. It was about the grace of the FATHER.

He looks down at his robe. He twirls the ring on his finger. He slaps his sandals against the floor, just like old times. Could it be? Could his sins be forgotten just because the father said so? Could there really be a future for him, even after all he had done? It seemed too good to be true.

That's grace.

Talk About It

1. Can you think of a time someone showed you grace when you didn't deserve it? How did it make you feel? How can you show grace to someone else?
2. Think about my story about my son's soccer game (and my crazy celebration) and the way God celebrates and loves you. What would you do differently if you knew that God is cheering you along the whole way?

3. How do Jesus' three parables—the lost coin, the lost sheep,
   and the prodigal son—explain why he was hanging out
   with people the Pharisees thought were bad news?

SIX

Grace Is a Person

When someone gives you a gift and says, "Go on, open it! I want to watch!" you should be nervous. In my experience, that's usually an indicator that something bizarre is about to go down. I'm sure you've been there. The person is certain you will love the gift. She can't wait to watch your reaction, which she expects to include but not be limited to tears, shouts of joy, and dancing in the streets.

So you open it. And you don't even know what it is.

"Oh, wow," you say. It's a nice, safe thing to say, and it buys you some time to regain control of your facial muscles.

"Do you love it?" she asks breathlessly.

"Of course! Yes! Wanted it. Loved it. Had to have it. How did you know?"

And when she leaves, you put it on a shelf in your closet, and you only bring it out when they come over, because you have no idea what to do with it.

Grace on the Shelf

That's what a lot of us end up doing with grace. We don't know what grace is or what to do with it, so we leave it on a shelf most of the time. Then we bring it out when we need to get ourselves out of trouble.

This shallow understanding leads some people to abuse grace. They sin on purpose. They plan ahead to sin. They know better—but they decide to do bad things anyway. Then they talk about grace and love and forgiveness when they get caught. For them, grace isn't about Jesus; it's just a spiritual-sounding way to weasel out of owning their actions. It's the ultimate Christian get-out-of-jail-free card.

People who flaunt their sin in the name of grace don't know what grace is. They don't know what to do with the gift they've been given, so they make it into something it isn't: a cover-up, a rug to sweep the nasty stuff under. That's not where grace belongs. That's like putting your bicycle in bed next to you. It doesn't belong there. It doesn't fit there.

But if we aren't careful, we can go to the other extreme. We see people who abuse grace, and it makes us scared of grace. We think that if we talk about God's love and mercy and forgiveness, people will try to get away with more sin. That's just plain wrong.

As I write about the grace and favor of God, about the overwhelming love that covers bad behavior and embraces bad people, I can hear the concerned voices in my mind: *He'd better not get too crazy with this grace thing. He'd better balance out that grace with some truth. He'd better make clear what he's saying. If he just preaches grace, people are going to start sinning.*

News flash: we are already sinning. We need grace to deal with the sin we already have.

Lately, I have realized something about grace that has changed my life. It's nothing new—people have understood this for years. It's straight out of the Bible. But it has become real to me, and it has helped a lot of things fall into place.

Grace is more than a principle, more than an idea, more than a cover-up for sin.

Grace is a person.

And his name is Jesus.

Oozing Grace

John, who was one of Jesus' disciples and closest friends, wrote this about Jesus: "We have seen his glory, glory as of the only Son from the Father, full of grace and truth . . . For from his fullness we have all received, grace upon grace. For the law was given through Moses; grace and truth came through Jesus Christ" (John 1:14–17 ESV).

There are several things to note in this short passage. First, Jesus was full of grace and truth. That means that grace and truth aren't enemies. They are on the same side. We don't need to balance grace with truth or truth with grace, because they are both found in Jesus. If we just get more of Jesus, we will have both grace and truth.

Second, this passage says that the grace Jesus brought replaces the grace Moses gave through the law. Jesus is saying rules are good and the law had its place. But really, the law isn't how we get to God. Grace is.

Most important, these verses say that Jesus was "full of grace and truth," and that from him we have received "grace upon grace." In other words, he embodied grace. He oozed grace. He *was* grace. After people met Jesus, they probably said things like, "That man is different. That man has grace all over him." Jesus gave people a picture of grace. They watched him and listened to him, and for the rest of their lives, they didn't have to wonder what grace looked like. They knew.

> Jesus is saying **RULES** are good and the **LAW** had its place. But really, the law isn't how we get to **GOD**. Grace is.

My favorite definition of grace is from Jack Hayford, a great pastor and author from San Fernando Valley, California: "Grace is God meeting us at our point of need in the Person of Jesus Christ." In other words, we need help, so God gives us grace. *And his name is Jesus.*

I'm not trying to repeat myself here—only to be clear. Jesus is the source of grace, the definition of grace, the home of grace. Jesus is grace, and grace is Jesus.

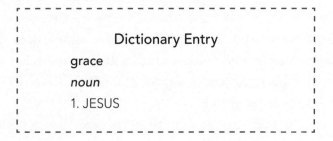

Dictionary Entry

grace

noun

1. JESUS

If you can picture Jesus, you can picture God. One of the most harmful things we do as humans is define God based on our own imagination. We come up with a few random ideas about what we think God is like, and we just assume we're right. Sometimes we mistakenly think that since God is our heavenly Father, he must be exactly like our earthly father. Not so. If we have trouble with parents, teachers, or adult authority figures, then we imagine that God is the same way, and we're going to have trouble with him too.

He embodied **GRACE.** He oozed grace. He **WAS** grace.

Some of us imagine God to be an angry God. We feel guilty for our bad deeds, and we know we would be mad at ourselves if we were in God's place, so we assume God must be furious.

And God is up in heaven asking, "Where did you get that idea of me? That's just wrong."

That's why Jesus came. He told his disciples, "Anyone who has seen me has seen the Father" (John 14:9). Jesus came to reveal the Father. He came to show us God. If you want to know what God thinks of you, or what God would say about your sin, or how God would respond if he were face-to-face with you, just look at Jesus, and you'll know.

God is up in **HEAVEN** asking, "Where did you get that **IDEA** of me? That's just **WRONG.**"

Grace Is a Person

When we realize that grace is a person, not a principle, abusing grace is no longer an option. It's easy to abuse a principle or to excuse away a doctrine. But it's much harder to abuse a person or violate a relationship.

For example, I have a lot of good friends, and you probably do too. I'm definitely not a perfect friend—sometimes I'm selfish, and sometimes I'm forgetful. Okay, almost all the time I'm forgetful.

But I'm also loyal. I care about my friends. I love them, and they love me.

If someone offered me a thousand dollars to somehow hurt or betray one of my friends, I would tell them to get lost, and I would probably say it in a not-very-nice way.

Why? Is it because I am loyal to some noble idea of friendship? Or because I am super self-controlled and I just force myself to do what a friend should do?

Not at all! I stay loyal to my friends because I know them. I have a relationship with them. I value them. I have lived life with them. The last thing I would want to do is hurt one of them, especially for something as dumb as money.

Remember, grace is not a concept. Grace is a person. Grace is Jesus.

When some people hear about grace, the first thing they think is: *So, I can go out and do whatever I want, and God has to forgive me?* They haven't met grace—they've met a concept. They've met an idea. They've heard a nice sermon.

When you look in the eyes of grace, when you meet grace, when you embrace grace, when you see the nail marks in grace's hands, when you feel his intense love for you—it will not motivate you to sin. It will motivate you to do what is right.

When we meet Jesus, grace becomes the fuel of our faith. We pray, we read our Bibles, we worship, and we live the purest lifestyle we can because we love a *person*. We'll do anything for someone we love.

Beware of Smurfs

The movie *The Smurfs* came out a while ago. If you haven't seen the movie or the old cartoon series it was based on, the storyline revolves around a bunch of tiny blue creatures called Smurfs who live in a magical land where they are constantly being chased by, and then outsmarting, a wizard named Gargamel and his cat. Standout memories include their irritating theme song and their use of the word *smurf* as every part of speech known to man.

"I smurf you."

"It's such a smurfy day."

"All the Smurfs are having a smurf of a time smurfily smurf- ing around the smurfity-smurf meadow."

And so on.

I was a kid in the eighties when the Smurfs first came out, and I remember that some of my friends were not allowed to watch the show. Why? Because there was a rumor going around that Smurfs were from the devil. People wrote books about it. Gargamel was a wizard, and there were spells and magic and a black cat, and supposedly Smurfs were little blue demons. So a lot of parents wouldn't let their kids watch the show because they wanted to protect them.

Were those parents right or wrong? It's not my place to decide. I think their motives were good: to protect and teach their children. I have kids now, and they don't always agree with my rules, but they still need to obey them.

My point isn't whether a certain TV show is okay to watch or not. My point is that sometimes we put too much trust in rules.

Rules are everywhere. There are rules at home, at school, at sports, at waterparks, and just about everywhere else. There are even signs in public restrooms telling you how to wash your hands. I'm sure your parents have rules for you, just like my parents had rules for me and just like I have rules for my kids.

Rules are not bad, but they can't save anyone. The best a rule or a law can do is draw a line and threaten to punish you if you cross that line. People still decide whether to obey the rule or not.

But there is something more effective than rules, and it's called relationship. It's called love.

> There IS something MORE effective than rules, and it's CALLED relationship. It's called LOVE.

My parents were much stricter than most parents I knew, but I didn't rebel. I didn't turn my back on God. I didn't feel like I had to go off and try out sin just to see if I liked it.

That doesn't mean I was a perfect child—I made more mistakes and dumb decisions than I like to remember. But overall, I respected and obeyed my dad and mom. And as I grew older and had more freedom, I found myself deciding on my own to do what I knew would please them.

Why? It wasn't because of rules. It wasn't because of threats. It certainly wasn't because I have such an easy-going personality—my parents and now my wife can tell you that.

It was because of relationship. My dad and mom loved me, and I loved them. So why would I *not* do what they asked?

I disagreed with their judgment calls sometimes. And I'm sure I was very vocal about it. But I never doubted their love for me. On some level, I realized their rules actually proved their love for me. Whether their decisions were right or wrong was less important than the motivation behind them.

> EVERYTHING that rules can do, GRACE can do better, and MORE besides.

I've watched people make rules out of fear. They try to use rules to guarantee their kids or their students or they themselves will never mess up. That doesn't work. That's not what rules are for. Rules are meant to lead us to relationship, not to replace relationship.

Let me throw out a word of caution. Focusing too much on rules and too little on grace tells people that what they do is more important than who they are.

Smurf on that for a while.

These principles aren't just about parents and kids. This is how our relationship with God works. For God, it's more about relationship than about rules. Far more.

Jesus proved that. He loved sinners—he loved us—long before we ever did anything to deserve it. Then he gave his life to pay for our sin so we could have an eternal relationship with God.

Here's the part that must bother God a bit. We take this grace-based, love-filled, amazing relationship, and we build a wall of rules around it. We turn relationship into religion. We make life more about us and about what we do or don't do than about God and his love.

Sure, we do it out of good hearts. We realize our sin sent Jesus to the cross, and we determine never to sin again. Ever, ever, ever. And we make up rules to keep ourselves far from the edge of sin.

Our solution is also our problem. Is "not sinning" really what it's all about? Is that God's top priority? When we get to heaven, is God going to check his celestial grade book and say, "It was close, but your holiness grade is better than the national average, so I'll let you in"?

When we see Jesus face-to-face, sin is going to be the furthest thing from our minds. All we will be thinking about is his grace and love and about how happy we are to be in his arms.

When we make up rules because we are afraid we or other people will sin, we end up missing the point of faith. It's not fear that saves us—it's faith. Fear of failure has a sneaky way of becoming a self-fulfilling prophecy, meaning that the more we are afraid of something, the more likely it is to happen. We focus so much on what we don't want to do that we end up doing it.

Make rules and follow rules as needed, but don't focus on rules. Focus on faith. Focus on grace. Focus on Jesus.

Here's the bottom line: everything that rules can do, grace can do better—and then some.

Rules I Would Have Made as a Kid

1. Raised my allowance to a thousand dollars a week.
2. Made it my parents' responsibility to clean my room.
3. Required teachers to raise their hands before speaking.

4. Made television a chore and homework optional.

5. Declared chips a vegetable.

Messy Grace

Believe it or not, rules are easier to deal with than grace. That's a big part of their attraction. That's why we keep making up rules even when we can't keep the ones we already have.

Rules are tidy. Grace is messy, unpredictable, and undeserved. I can hold my life up against a set of rules and decide if I'm a good person or a bad person. I can do the same with your life, without the messiness of getting to know you or understanding what you're going through.

Not so with grace. Grace risks its reputation to eat with notorious sinners. It sacrifices its schedule to help hurting people. Grace doesn't allow us the luxury of being separate from people. It doesn't get so distracted with doing good things that it forgets about people.

> **GRACE** doesn't get so distracted with doing **GOOD** things that it forgets about **PEOPLE.**

If you choose to live by grace and not by rules, you are in for some messy moments. You'll have to decide what is right and wrong based on what God wants, not on some set of rules someone made up. You'll have to love and accept people who don't act like you think they should, rather than only hanging out with people you are comfortable with. You'll have to give people room to fail instead of rejecting them when they mess up.

But once you've embraced grace, you'll never let go.

Talk About It

1. You just read that Jesus was *full of grace and truth*, and that when people met him they must have thought, *That man is different. That man has grace all over him.* How does being full of grace and truth make a person different? How does it change how a person acts?

2. What do you think God thinks of you? What does grace have to do with that?

3. Name some rules you have to follow that are there to help you. Have you ever broken a rule and been shown grace? What was that time like?

4. What's the point of having rules? What's the point of grace?

SEVEN

Worthy World

Many of us spend all our time in what I call Worthy World. It's kind of like Disneyland. Disneyland's motto is "The happiest place on earth." Worthy World's motto is "You only get what you deserve." That's the first thing they tell you when you check in. It's posted on all the walls. It's playing on loudspeakers all day long.

Worthy World is lame. The paint is peeling on all the attractions. The Ferris wheel is twelve feet tall and gets stuck all the time. Your neck hurts after riding the bumper cars because they jerk so badly. The petting zoo features a scrawny goat and a dog that looks as if it might have rabies. The popcorn is a week old and tastes like burnt grease.

Many of us are still riding the pathetic little rides at Worthy World. We wonder why it isn't more fun, but we can't afford anything else. So we laugh empty laughs and tell each other how great this place is.

And every once in a while, over the fence we catch a glimpse of an amazing place called Grace Land. Grace Land is full of the craziest, most awesome rides ever. We see people who are having the time of their lives on these enormous roller coasters. We look over from our little carousel and wonder what they did to get into Grace Land.

Wow, we think. *Tickets to that park must cost a fortune. I could never get in there. I could never earn that.*

Then someone peers through a hole in the Worthy World fence and says, "Dude, why don't you come over to Grace Land? It's awesome! It's amazing!"

"No, I can't do that. I could never pay for that. I don't deserve that. Grace is not for me."

"Don't you know? Grace Land is free!"

"Free? No, that's not possible. That's too good to be true. Thanks anyway. I only take what I deserve."

That sounds like humility, but it's not. It's false humility, which is just pride dressed up as modesty. Pride is one of the greatest enemies of grace.

Pride says, "I can do this on my own. I want to earn what I get. I want to brag about what I've done on my own."

Humility says, "I need help. I'm willing to admit it. I'm willing to accept assistance. I don't have anything to prove."

You thought Disneyland was expensive? At Worthy World, they'll charge everything you can cough up, and it still won't be enough. But the rides at Grace Land won't cost you a thing. Jesus owns the park, and he says that anyone who wants can come in at no charge.

We don't have to earn anything. We don't have to pay anything. We don't have to deserve anything. That's what grace is all about.

Lamest Rules at Worthy World

1. No screaming on roller coasters.
2. Under no circumstances may bumper cars run into each other.
3. All snacks must be whole wheat.
4. Must wear a tuxedo on all water slides.
5. Port-A-Potties are five dollars a turn, and there is only one for the entire park.

Finished

Say it's Christmas, and your parents just bought you something that you really wanted—maybe a new game console or some expensive shoes. You are sitting there, enjoying your gift, and they are having fun seeing how excited you are. But suddenly you get a sad look on your face. You look at them and say, "Dad, Mom—thanks for this, but I just don't deserve it. It's too much. I'm not worth that. I'm going to pay you back for this."

How would they feel? First of all, they'd probably pass out from shock. But when they sat back up, they would feel a little hurt. They love you and want to bless you, so why would you try to pay them back? It's rude. It's ungrateful. It's even a little insulting.

I doubt it has ever entered your mind to try to repay your

parents for your Christmas presents. It never entered my mind when I was a kid. That's for sure. But sometimes we treat God's gifts this way.

Some people think that when they receive God's grace to cover their sins, they are taking advantage of him. They know they were saved by grace at first, but they feel as though every new sin is another nail in Jesus' hands. When they mess up and have to ask for forgiveness, they do it with the feeling that they are frustrating God or insulting his generosity.

I respect their sincerity and work ethic, but they are dead wrong.

Grace wasn't free for Jesus. It cost him everything. That is exactly why we should receive it freely. The most insulting thing we could do is reject this costly gift and say, "No thanks, God, I got this." Please don't tell me Jesus was put up on the cross so we could try to save ourselves through our wimpy good deeds. Don't insult Jesus' sacrifice by trying to pay him back.

When we receive and enjoy his grace, we aren't bothering God. Far from it. That's how he likes it. In God's mind, Jesus' death on the cross solved the sin problem, and now we can get back to the amazing life God originally created for us.

I find the more I get to know Jesus and his goodness, the more I want to live in a way that pleases him. It's that simple.

Sometimes we get too focused on how strong sin is and how easily we do bad things. We worry that if we relax for a second, we'll mess up and ruin everything.

Then someone comes along and tells us about grace. They tell us God loves us no matter what. They say God isn't nearly as worried about our sin as we are, because Jesus already dealt with sin on the cross. And we think, *I already mess up a lot. If*

I stop stressing over being good, who knows what will become of me. So we hold our holiness in a death grip and we strive for perfection as if it all depends on our performance.

It doesn't. That's the point. That's what Jesus was saying to the crowds, and to his disciples, and to notorious sinners, and to the Pharisees. Our status with Jesus doesn't depend on what we do, but what Jesus already did for us.

One of the last things Jesus said as he hung on the cross has been ringing in my mind lately. It is a phrase that changed forever how man relates to God, and it has altered the way I view myself, the way I understand God, and the way I react to sin.

> JESUS said, "It is FINISHED."

Jesus said, "It is finished" (John 19:30).

The more I think about this important little phrase, the more convinced I am that we need a bigger idea of God and a smaller idea of sin. Some of us are so overwhelmed by what's wrong about us that we can't believe Jesus could love us. That's a problem. That's a far bigger problem than the sin itself.

In some ways, sin is a big deal. But it's not as big a deal as it used to be, and it won't be a big deal at all in the future. Let me explain.

Sin is a big deal when you consider that all sin is rebellion against God. It is a big deal when you realize we are often slaves to our sin, doing things we really don't want to do because something inside us controls us. It is a big deal when you look around the world and see all the pain and suffering sin causes. And it is a big deal when you realize that death exists because sin exists.

But sin's days are numbered. Evil is on its way out. Jesus'

death dealt with the guilt of sin and the power of sin. As we walk with him, we will sin less, and so the effects of sin will lessen too.

Before Jesus, all people could do was try their hardest and offer sacrifices to (sort of) make up for their guilt. They would kill sheep and birds and bulls as symbols of how serious sin was and how guilty they were.

That sounds scary to us these days, but it was the best they could do. You might be wondering, *What good did it do to kill an animal? How could an animal's death make up for their mistakes?*

Exactly.

That's why they had to offer sacrifices all the time—daily, weekly, monthly, yearly. And even with all that, they still never dealt with the heart of the issue: their own sinful nature.

The sacrifices were meant to remind people they needed a solution for sin. Ultimately, the sacrifices pointed to Jesus.

Hebrews 10:11–14 says, "The priest stands and ministers before the altar day after day, offering the same sacrifices again and again, which can never take away sins. But our High Priest offered himself to God as a single sacrifice for sins, good for all time. . . . For by that one offering he forever made perfect those who are being made holy."

Jesus was the ultimate sacrifice. His death was sufficient for all sin, for all time. It replaced the ineffective and insufficient animal sacrifices of the past.

Once again, is sin a big deal? Considering all the above, I have to say not anymore. The problem has been solved. The solution has been provided. The answer has been found. His name is Jesus, and he is full of grace.

Simple Jesus

Whether we choose to use God's provision for sin is another matter, of course. And some of the power and the effects of sin will only be fully erased when Jesus returns and deals with sin and evil once and for all. But Jesus is enough. Jesus is sufficient.

Jesus brings hope for a needy world, and it's called grace. "Where sin abounded," the Bible says, "grace abounded much more" (Romans 5:20 NKJV). Jesus didn't come to condemn the world; he came to save the world. If he thinks there is hope, if he believes in humanity, we should too.

Jesus' solution to sin was his own death and resurrection, and that is where our hope for the world must be placed. We shouldn't put our trust in our efforts to be good, or in education, or in the government. It seems most of Seattle can't even navigate a traffic jam without flipping out, so thinking we can achieve world peace by trying harder or educating people is a bit foolish. Those things are helpful, but they aren't the answer.

Jesus is.

> His GRACE is available to ANYONE who wants it. No restrictions. No LIMITS. No conditions.

We have to realize that there is more to life than sin. How much of our lives revolves around sin? Everything wrong with this world, from war to famine to sickness, is a consequence of sin. If we didn't have to deal with sin, how much further along would the human race be?

This book is a manifesto of sorts. It is a simple call to return to a simple faith in a simple person. Jesus *is* the gospel. He is the core of Christianity. His grace is available to anyone who wants it. No restrictions. No limits. No conditions.

> ### Dictionary Entry
> ma-nə-ˈfes-tō
> *noun*
> 1. a public declaration of intentions or views

When Jesus died on the cross, he provided a way for us to access God. He solved the sin problem. He paid for the sins of anyone who chooses to accept him.

> God isn't just **WILLING** to forgive sinners—he is **PASSIONATE** about it.

As I think about the depth of God's grace and the meaning it has for each of us, I get overwhelmed. God isn't just *willing* to forgive sinners—he is *passionate* about it. Even when we were enemies, even before we had done anything to deserve his love, even though he knew we would sin, he still loved us. Nothing can compare to that grace.

I don't pretend to understand the answer to every question about God and life. Honestly, no one can. You can't calculate the size of infinite love. You can't fit it into a mathematical formula.

But you can meet Jesus. He is the personification of grace. His death on the cross and his resurrection from the dead three days later are the ultimate demonstrations of that grace.

We would do well to stop focusing on our sins, our failures, our weaknesses, things that happened in the past, and our rule-crazy attempts to live perfectly, and simply enjoy the finished work of Jesus. That is where grace is found. That is where we receive forgiveness for the past and power to live differently in the present.

Grace is so simple that we have a hard time believing it could be true. But I'm convinced that unless it's too good to be true, it's not grace.

So let's not focus on the bad stuff. It doesn't help to tell ourselves, *Don't think about the bad stuff. Don't think about gossiping. Don't think about smoking. Don't think about—*

That's not really the point. Yes, we should avoid thinking about sin. But trying not to think about something is the surest way to keep thinking about it.

That's why you have to be a master of distraction if there is a toddler in your family. If you have a brother or sister who's around two years old, I'm sure you've figured this out. For example, you never want to just tell a toddler, "Don't put my iPad in the potty." If that's all you say, he'll stand there, staring at the toilet, thinking about the glorious splash your iPad will make.

> **Unless it's TOO good to be true, it's not GRACE.**

So you close the lid, you shut the door, you hide the iPad, and—key point here—you give him something else to do. Show him something constructive that doesn't involve toilets and tablets. Because as long as he's thinking about what he's not supposed to do, chances are very high that he'll figure out how to do it.

Here's what I'm trying to say: the point isn't to quit thinking about sin. It's to quit thinking about self and instead to think about Jesus. It's to become God-conscious, not me-conscious.

Are you struggling with sin? You don't need more willpower. You need more of Jesus.

Loving Jesus, not avoiding sin, is the focal point of our lives.

Yearbook Day

I graduated from Issaquah High School in 1997. At that point it was the largest high school in the state of Washington, with about twenty-two hundred students.

One of my favorite days in high school was yearbook day. I don't know how your school does this, but when we got our yearbooks, they gave us a half day to go around and sign everybody's yearbook. I loved yearbook day—whatever it takes to get people to say nice things about me.

I was well liked, but I remember at times being avoided by some people, even by some of my basketball teammates. I didn't really know why. Maybe they thought I was dorky or weird, or maybe they thought I was cooler than them and they were intimidated by me. I hoped it was the second.

On yearbook day, I exchanged yearbooks with a couple of dozen people, and then I went home and spent two hours reading what people had to say about me. I was shocked as I read what certain people thought about me. I remember thinking, *If I had known they thought this highly of me, I would have been even bolder to share the love of Jesus.*

I still have my yearbook, and recently I read through it

again. What can I say—I guess it's still all about me! Anyway, I remember these guys, and I remember how they acted as if I never existed. And I'm still amazed at what was going on in their heads that whole year of silence.

One guy wrote, "Judah, you're truly the most extraordinary young man I've ever met."

What? High school guys don't talk to each other like that.

He continued, "You're an inspiration to me and all Christians alike. I have the utmost respect for you. Your daily devotion and love for Jesus helps everybody around you."

FYI, this guy never talked to me. Never. I thought I was dead to him. He wasn't serving Jesus in high school until the very end. But he watched me from a distance and looked up to me. If only I had known, I would have been a lot less insecure.

Here's another one: "Judah, you're probably the person I respect most at this school."

I wish you knew this guy. This is unbelievable.

He continues, "You have your beliefs and you stick to them. That's awesome."

Wow. It wasn't awesome when I sat by myself sometimes in the lunchroom. Didn't feel awesome.

"I'm so glad we spent time together."

I'm trying to remember when that was. I tried to, but he was never available to hang out.

"I hope we can hang out or go golfing this summer. Give me a call if you need a fourth for golf. You're one heck of a quarterback too. Sophomore football was fun. I've learned a lot from you, and thanks for everything you've done for me. Friends for life."

I remember sitting at home in my bedroom reading my yearbook, looking at the names and pictures, thinking, *There is no way this person thinks that.* Had I known they respected me, had I known so-and-so thought I was the most extraordinary young man he had ever met, I would have walked through the halls like a more extraordinary person.

I wonder what God would say if he could write in our yearbooks. I think most of us, when we think of God scribbling his perspective of us in our yearbooks, expect what I expected from my friends: "Hey, you're an okay guy." "You're kind of weird." "Dude, leave me alone." "Get a life." "Get your act together."

Things God Might Write in Your Yearbook

1. You make me smile! I love being part of your life.
2. You're perfect, and I wouldn't change a thing about you.
3. Remember that one day when you flushed your locker key and had your PE shorts on backward and accidentally texted the principal instead of your secret crush? Hilarious. I think you're amazing anyway.
4. Guess what? I know your future. And it's awesome.
5. Um, there's something stuck in your teeth.
6. Nice yearbook picture. Hahahaha! Just kidding. You'll grow out of those things that are bugging you.
7. I love you more than you could ever know.

There is a way for us to get God's perspective of us. It's called the Bible—but most of the time we skim the grace parts and highlight the sin parts.

If Jesus wrote in your yearbook, I think you would be blown away by what he really thinks about you. I think you would live differently because Jesus is crazy about you. He is obsessed with you. He is proud of you.

This understanding could literally help your posture. It could help you walk with your head held high. If you think the God of the galaxies is ticked at you, you're probably going to be a bit depressed.

"Hey, man, what's wrong?"

"Oh, the Creator of everything is furious with me. He might kill me any second."

Well, I'd be depressed too. That's a weight to carry if I ever heard of one.

Contrary to popular opinion, God is not mad at us. Yes, we can hurt God. We can grieve God. But his wrath against sin was erased by Jesus' death. For those who accept that sacrifice by faith, he no longer looks at our sin. When he sees us, he sees his Son.

When Jesus was baptized, God shouted down for all to hear, "You are my dearly loved Son, and you bring me great joy" (Luke 3:22).

God is just as pleased with us as he is with his Son.

That's not exaggeration. That's not blasphemy. It's the truth. It's the Bible. John wrote, "Love has been perfected among us in this: that we may have boldness in the day of judgment; because as He is, so are we in this world" (1 John 4:17 NKJV).

In other words, when God sees us, he sees Jesus. We have the same status before God as Jesus. We aren't God, of course,

> If JESUS wrote in your YEARBOOK, I think you would be blown AWAY by what he really THINKS about you.

so there is a difference. But when it comes to our righteousness, we are just as pure as Jesus.

Grace is a difficult concept for us humans to embrace because we have to live with ourselves. We are painfully aware of our weaknesses and mistakes. So we are usually hardest on ourselves. It's amazing how many people can accept others but are still trying to find a way to accept themselves.

Sometimes our brains are our own worst enemies because grace isn't logical. It doesn't work on a cause-and-effect basis like everything else in life. You've heard about cause and effect in science. For every effect, there has to have been a cause. An apple falls. That's an effect. *There must be a cause*, thought Sir Newton. And he discovered gravity.

The other day I was teaching a class at my church, and I fell off the platform. I have a bad habit of standing with my feet half off the edge. People make fun of me for it, but in fifteen-plus years of preaching that way, I had never fallen. This particular day I was leaning forward to read a verse that was up on a monitor, and gravity took over. It was a graceful fall, as falls go, and the only damage was a sprain in my pride. Cause: gravity and clumsiness. Effect: I fell off the platform. It's a law of nature.

> When GOD sees us, he sees JESUS.

When it comes to grace, though, there's just effect, at least as far as humans are concerned. We didn't do anything to cause it. It's already been caused, and we should just enjoy it. But that bothers us because we feel like there should be a cause. Because logic gets in the way, we try to figure grace out. We try to find a reason why we deserved it.

Grace, though, is supernatural by definition, so it is bigger than anything we can understand with our human brains. God's ways are higher than our ways. His thoughts are higher than our thoughts. He is God and we are not.

Talk About It

1. When have you ever felt like an outsider—like someone at Worthy World looking in on Grace Land? How does it feel to know that you are never an outsider to God?

2. Has anyone ever written or said anything surprising about you in a yearbook-type situation? What do you think God would write in your yearbook that's specific to you?

3. How is Jesus the solution to the sin problem? According to this chapter, what does he do to the guilt, the power, and the effect of sin?

Jesus Is THE POINT.

EIGHT

Come to Me

This isn't a very spiritual thing to admit, but I like to sleep. A lot. Rest and relaxation are high on my priority scale.

This is especially true in the morning. I know pastors who absolutely love early-morning prayer meetings. By "early morning," I mean before the Holy Spirit is even awake. They get up, get dressed, get breakfast, and get to church by six o'clock in the morning, and they have the sweetest, most spiritual attitudes as they lead their people in prayer.

At six in the morning, I am of no use to God or anyone else. Except for maybe the devil, because I act more like him than anyone else at that ungodly hour. My idea of an early-morning prayer meeting is ten in the morning.

I've been in more churches than you've been in McDonald's. I always hear preachers say things like, "I was up at five thirty this morning just praying and reading my Bible, and it was awesome."

And I'm thinking, *Man, I'm sure not as holy as that guy.*

Because if anyone tried to wake me up that early, I'd yell things at them that would shock my mama. I know I would.

If I had my way, the world would not begin in the hours that have single digits. The single digits are for my wife and me, for our kids, for breakfast, for time alone with God and family and self. I will see you at ten o'clock or later, and I will be a holy man, just as you expect.

I get asked a lot, "Judah, what's your favorite verse in the Bible?"

I always get a bit suspicious, because maybe it's a trick question. Maybe my favorite verse isn't as good as your favorite verse. Inside I'm wondering, *I don't know, what should it be? You go first.*

Common-Sense Sleep Guidelines

1. No one gets up before 10:00 a.m.
2. Mothers do not wake children by flinging open curtains to reveal the blinding sunshine.
3. There is no talking at breakfast.
4. The phrase "Well, if you had gone to bed earlier . . ." shall never be uttered.
5. "Just five more minutes" is a valid request and must be honored.

Here's a question I never get asked: "What's your least favorite verse?" I've actually thought about that. Maybe I'm on thin ice here, because it's the Bible, and we are supposed to like all the verses. But I can tell you exactly what my least favorite scripture in the entire Bible is. It's Proverbs 20:13: "Do not love sleep, lest you come to poverty. Open your eyes, and you will be satisfied with bread" (NKJV).

That's my least favorite verse. I'm sorry. But I bet you can relate, so don't judge!

I also don't like the passage that says Jesus got up a long while before daybreak and went and prayed. Really? What did he have to go and do that for? He was God. Couldn't he just sleep in and encourage us mortals a bit?

So, I like sleep. I don't love it, because the Bible says not to. I just like it. A lot.

Proverbs has another verse on sleep, and this one is more to my liking. Proverbs 3:24 says, "You can go to bed without fear; you will lie down and sleep soundly." That's the verse I'm holding on to.

Lawmakers and Lawbreakers

Actually, rest is a good thing. Sometimes we get so super spiritual and wound up about life, and what we really need is some rest. If some of us got more sleep, we'd be more like Jesus.

One of my favorite passages in the Bible has to do with rest. It does more than just encourage us to take naps though; this passage teaches us about a spiritual rest. Spiritual rest means being free from worry, fear, and stress. These verses have revolutionized how I think. They are found in Matthew 11:28–30.

Then Jesus said, "Come to me, all of you who are weary and carry heavy burdens, and I will give you rest. Take my yoke upon you. Let me teach you, because I am humble and gentle at heart, and you will find rest for your souls. For my yoke is easy to bear, and the burden I give you is light."

When Jesus spoke these words, he was talking to crowds of people who had grown up under the Jewish religious system. This was a system defined by law. People related to God based on law. They related to each other based on law. They worked and raised their families and lived their day-to-day lives based on law.

When we think of the term *law* today, we think of government-required limits. But to Israel, law meant more than not driving your camel too fast in a school zone. It referred to the law of Moses.

Around fifteen hundred years earlier, God, through Moses, gave the Israelites a series of laws that dealt with religious, moral, and practical issues. These laws were designed to help Israel maintain a high moral standard. Israel was surrounded by nations that practiced terrible, violent things like human sacrifice, so the law was God's way to help people live better lives.

The most famous of these laws were the Ten Commandments, but that was only the start. The law of Moses was much more detailed than that. It affected every area of life. The Israelites were commanded to keep this law down to the smallest detail, and if they failed in any way, they were guilty of sin. Because no one could keep all the law all the time, they had to offer continual animal sacrifices for sin, as I mentioned earlier.

To make matters worse, in the centuries leading up to Jesus, the Jews had added several hundred additional laws to the law of Moses. This body of laws, much of which was tradition, was meant to help people fulfill the original law of Moses by controlling their daily lives even more. It was an incredibly detailed set of rules, and it was the Pharisees' self-appointed duty to explain and apply this law to everybody's lives.

In past chapters, we discussed rule-based living as opposed to grace-based living. This is exactly where Israel had ended up. That wasn't God's idea when he gave them the law—it was just human nature.

You Look Tired

I hate it when people tell me, "Judah, you look tired." That's another way of telling me I look terrible.

"Gee, thanks!" I wish I could say. "You look terrible too!" But I'm a pastor, and pastors don't tell people in their congregations they look bad.

Have you ever felt like it's way too much work to do everything you're supposed to do? I don't just mean going to school, doing homework, participating in sports, going to family events, guarding your room from your siblings, helping friends who are going through dating drama, and going to church. I'm talking more about your attitude and your behavior. I'm talking about the effort it takes to be nice, be generous, be happy, and be respectful while you are doing all of the above activities. That's not easy. Sometimes it can feel overwhelming, especially when you try really hard to do what's right and you fail again and again.

When Jesus came on the scene, people were stressed out

and worn out trying to please God. They were so busy trying to do good in order to be good that they couldn't see how good life was. They couldn't enjoy God because they never quite measured up—they always needed a little more holiness and a few more good deeds before God could accept them.

They saw God as a lawmaker, a judge, a law enforcer, a cosmic policeman who was obsessed with keeping people in line. That was why, as we discussed earlier, people reacted so strongly to Jesus hanging out with sinners. He claimed to be God, yet he didn't slap handcuffs on anyone. He didn't hand out parking tickets or death sentences. He just loved people, and he offered them full and free access to God.

When Jesus said, "I will give you rest," people gasped. It was like the feeling of relief and relaxation you get when your mom tells you to go back to sleep because it snowed the night before and school is canceled. Your sleep is always the sweetest when you thought you had to get up but you ended up getting the day off.

The people listening to Jesus could hardly believe it was true.

"Rest? Really? What does he mean? I thought serving God was hard work?"

Sometimes we think the same thing. We think it's too hard to be good. It's too hard to obey. It's too hard to have a good attitude. It's too hard to resist temptations at school. It's too hard to love bullies.

Jesus says the same thing to us that he said the people listening so long ago: he is our source of rest. It's not about working harder: it's about discovering inner peace with God through Jesus.

The "Discussion" on the Mount

When I was in school, I was definitely not an A+ student. I was about as far from that as you can get. I actually had to take pre-algebra three times before I passed. My favorite parts of school involved hanging out with friends and sports—neither of which ends up on your report card. Books and tests and homework just didn't excite me.

Some of my friends would get upset if they got an A instead of an A+. They'd be up front asking the teacher for extra credit so they could take their grade from 98 to 100. Sorry, but I just couldn't understand that. I was perfectly happy with a C in any class. That was average. That was acceptable. That was a passing grade.

Hold that thought—I'll come back to it.

When Jesus told the people he was the ultimate source of rest, I think something clicked in their minds. You see, this wasn't the first time he had talked to them about burdens and law. But the previous time, he wasn't nearly so encouraging. Backtrack to Matthew chapter 5.

Matthew 5 is the beginning of Jesus' most famous sermon. It is called the Sermon on the Mount because he preached it from a mountainside so the crowds could hear him better.

This particular part could have been called the "discussion" on the Mount. Like when your parents say they need to "discuss" something with you, but you do very little of the talking. Something is clearly bugging Jesus. He says:

> "Don't misunderstand why I have come. I did not come to
> abolish the law of Moses or the writings of the prophets. No,
> I came to accomplish their purpose. I tell you the truth, until

heaven and earth disappear, not even the smallest detail of God's law will disappear until its purpose is achieved. So if you ignore the least commandment and teach others to do the same, you will be called the least in the Kingdom of Heaven. But anyone who obeys God's laws and teaches them will be called great in the Kingdom of Heaven.

But I warn you—unless your righteousness is better than the righteousness of the teachers of religious law and the Pharisees, you will never enter the Kingdom of Heaven!" (vv. 17–20)

He had their attention now. Who could possibly be more righteous than the religious teachers and the Pharisees? They were the definition of religiousness, the example of perfect behavior. And they let everybody know it too.

This would be like finding out you had to get a better grade than the brainiest kid in school on every test, in every assignment, in every class. It's not going to happen.

The common, everyday guy was shaking his head right about now. *Righteousness that is greater than that of the Pharisees? I'm in trouble.*

Jesus is just getting warmed up. I won't quote the rest of the chapter here, but it's strong stuff. Jesus breaks down what it means to be righteous and perfect on a practical, day-to-day level.

His message could have been subtitled "But I Say." He goes through a list of topics, and for each one, he starts out, "You have heard . . . ," and then he quotes a commonly known law. Then he follows with, "but I say," and he basically says that what they had been taught—though it was strict—wasn't strict enough. God wanted more.

These were more than pet peeves. Jesus wasn't being picky. He wasn't having a bad day. He had grown up in this culture, and he knew how people got around God's commandments. He had seen them justify their unfairness and excuse their sin with shallow, religious-sounding arguments.

It was like me at school: I knew I could get by with a C. I felt okay about my school performance because at least I was passing (well, most of the time anyway). Why work harder? I was fine. I would make it through.

> These were **MORE** than pet peeves. Jesus wasn't being **PICKY.**

The people of Jesus' day were trusting in the good things they were doing, thinking those things were enough to keep God happy. They knew they weren't perfect, but they figured they were okay. They would make it through. They would pass.

Jesus wanted them to understand something though. A few good deeds were not enough. God wanted perfection. And since no one was perfect, these people were in trouble. They needed help.

Spoiler alert: they needed Jesus.

But he didn't come right out and say that. Instead, he stands on a mountain and calls them out for their "I'm good enough" attitude. He tells them that if they aren't getting an A+, if they aren't perfect in every way, they might as well be getting an F.

He starts out, "You have heard it said, 'Do not murder.'"

And everyone is thinking, *I'm good on this one. I haven't murdered anyone. Wanted to, maybe, but never did. I'm good. I'm off the hook.*

Jesus continues, "But I say, if you are even mad at someone, you deserve judgment."

The crowd gets silent. Awkwardly silent. And then probably someone's cell phone rings, because that's what always happens.

What? people are thinking. *I can't even get mad at my neighbor? Clearly Jesus doesn't know my neighbor.*

Jesus continues. He's relentless, direct. He touches on family, on divorce, on revenge, on enemies. Each time he points out that even if they thought they were righteous, they were only fooling themselves.

He finishes with, "You have heard it said, 'Love your neighbor but hate your enemy,' but I say, love your enemies and pray for those who persecute you."

"What?" They look at each other. "Pray for bullies? I'll pray, all right—*Lord, destroy them all!*" That's my prayer. What's he talking about? Love them? That's crazy."

People are not shouting Jesus down during this sermon. They are not yelling "Amen" or waving their handkerchiefs. By this point, they have figured out that the "But I Say" discussion is not a feel-good sermon. It is not encouraging. In fact, it is downright depressing.

And in case someone made it through the message without having his or her self-righteousness rocked, Jesus caps it off by saying, "But you are to be perfect, even as your Father in heaven is perfect."

There is a rousing round of silence. People are thinking, *It was hard enough to be righteous before. I could barely keep up with everything the Pharisees told me do to. But this? This is impossible.*

Exactly.

That was the point.

Obsessed

Jesus wanted them to know that if they intended to live by the law, they couldn't just pick and choose the parts they liked in order to feel good about themselves. They had to follow all the law or they might as well not follow any of it.

Jesus wasn't being mean. He was showing them their own inconsistencies. In their hurry to be good, they had changed what it meant to be holy so they could fulfill the law on their own. They had moved the goalposts closer. They had convinced themselves that they were okay, that they would at least get a passing grade. They had fooled themselves into thinking they didn't need help.

The biggest problem with that was not that they were still sinning. God was used to that. It was that they thought they were good to go. They thought they were good enough to get into heaven on their own, just by following rules. (At least the "good" people thought this—the "sinners," as we saw in the first chapter, had given up long ago.) Self-righteousness is one of the biggest things that blocks us from having a relationship with God.

> They THOUGHT the point was being GOOD and doing good. But it WASN'T.

Bottom line: they had missed the point of the law. They thought the point was being good and doing good. But it wasn't.

The point was that we all need Jesus.

Deep inside, people knew they weren't righteous anyway. They knew they needed another way. It was never possible to fulfill the law. Jesus wanted them to come to the end of themselves so they could discover the grace that God freely offered through Jesus.

God knew Israel could never keep the whole law. The law was not meant to perfect people, just to lead them toward a perfect God.

For Israel, the law was never meant to be about the law. It was about Jesus. It pointed to Jesus. In John 5:39, Jesus says to the Pharisees, "You search the Scriptures because you think they give you eternal life. But the Scriptures point to me!"

Jesus was the fulfillment of the law. That's why he could say he came to accomplish the purpose of the law. All the law, the prophecies, and the teachings that the Israelites studied day in and day out pointed to Jesus.

God wanted people to do their best, of course, but ultimately he wanted them to know they needed a Savior, a Messiah.

> He WANTED them to KNOW they needed a SAVIOR, a Messiah.

The same principles hold true today. God doesn't want us to just try harder, work harder, and get busier. He appreciates our efforts, but when we make life about doing good and being better, when we make holiness an end in itself, we miss the point.

Being a Christian is not about being good. It's about relationship. About grace. About Jesus. He is the point of life.

I've heard Christians talk about the "be perfect" verse we just looked at, and they say, "See? With Jesus, the requirements are even higher than under the law. So you better get busy. Be a better person. Try harder. You have a long way to go."

It's amazing to me that sometimes we leave church more obsessed with ourselves than when we came in. That should never be the result of the gospel. When you've heard the gospel, you get obsessed with Jesus, because it points to him.

The times I fail, I could get totally discouraged and think I am not worthy to be a pastor. Or I could realize the truth that I was never worthy in the first place. It's not about me. It's about God, about grace, and about helping people in my church and my city meet Jesus.

This is what's crazy. Sometimes, when we do something wrong, we try to do something for God to feel like we are paying for our sin. It's less embarrassing that way. We don't feel so in debt to grace.

But it's useless and unnecessary. Why insist on paying for what Jesus already bought?

I don't want to pretend I am holier than anyone. I want to start resting in the righteousness Jesus gives me. Don't get me wrong—I'm not saying we should care less about holiness. I'm saying we should care more about Jesus.

> I was NEVER worthy in the first PLACE. It's not about me. It's about GOD.

When we put our faith in Jesus, we are made righteous. We can't work hard enough to get an A+ at life, but we don't have to. Jesus already did. And he makes us perfect, holy, righteous. I will never be more righteous than I am today. God will never love me more than he does right now.

That's amazing.

Infinity Times Infinity

When God looks at me, he says, "That man is righteous." That's just who I am, and I can't change who I am. Even if I haven't prayed in six days, I am righteous. Even if I'm struggling with sin, I am righteous. Even if I don't feel righteous, I am righteous.

Some of us need to go out and get a stamp made that says RIGHTEOUS, and every morning we need to stamp our foreheads with it. Get it made backward so that when we look in the mirror we can read it. Like so:

RIGHTEOUS

Our good deeds are good, and God is proud of them, and they make the world a better place. So by all means, don't stop doing them. Just don't trust in them for righteousness. That takes the fun out of everything.

Jesus is infinitely righteous, and we are as righteous as he is. So any attempt to make ourselves more righteous by our good deeds would be like trying to one-up infinity.

Remember that reasoning from when you were a little kid?

Maybe you were arguing with your brother about who was the smartest. "I'm a thousand times smarter than you."

"Well, I'm a million times smarter than you."

"I'm infinity times smarter."

"Oh yeah? I'm infinity plus one times smarter."

"Actually, I'm infinity plus a million. Plus one."

> In God's EYES we are perfect. Just like JESUS.

"I'm infinity times infinity. Ha! You can't beat that!"

We don't need to play that game. If we have faith in Jesus and his work on the cross, then we are as righteous right now as we ever need to be. We can't add to it, and we can't take away from it.

We are righteous enough to walk into heaven, right up to God's throne, and ask him for whatever we need. That's not what I say—that's what the Bible says. "So let us come boldly to the throne of our gracious God. There we will receive his mercy, and we will find grace to help us when we need it most" (Hebrews 4:16).

Proverbs says that a righteous man may fall seven times, but he rises again. Did you catch that? He's righteous, yet he falls. It's not his perfect track record that made him righteous. The guy fell seven times. He's a klutz. He's a failure.

The man is righteous because God said he's righteous. He's righteous because he trusts God to make him righteous. And because he knows he's righteous, he attempts great things, crazy things, and he never gives up.

> We are as **RIGHTEOUS** right now as we ever **NEED** to be. We can't **ADD** to it, and we can't take **AWAY** from it.

We get in such a hurry to perfect ourselves because we think that as soon as we do, God will love us more. But he will never love us more than he does right now. He will never accept us more than he does right now.

God is not in a hurry to fix us. Our behavior is not his first priority. We are his first priority. Loving us is his main concern.

Our fight against sin is noble and good, but make no

mistake: we are not fighting to become righteous. We are already righteous. It's who we are. Sure, we don't always act like it, and we still sin more than we should, but in God's eyes, we are perfect. Just like Jesus.

Talk About It

1. What is your favorite—or your least favorite—Bible verse? Why?

2. Does it ever feel like hard work to be good and to please God? What is hard about it? How does understanding Jesus help you be at rest and peace even when you make mistakes?

3. What has your perception of God been in the past? How does knowing who Jesus is change your view of God and your relationship with him?

NINE

The Meaning of Life

It's not just adults who wonder about the meaning of life. Maybe you've asked yourself, *Why am I here? What is life all about? What will make me happy as I grow up?*

Maybe it was late at night. You couldn't sleep, and you started to think about the meaning of life.

People everywhere wonder about the purpose of life, but they can't agree on the answer. Is life about love? Is it about having the latest smartphone or laptop? Is it about getting married one day and having children of your own? Is it about having a pet? Is it about having friends? Is it about vacations? Is it about making straight As in school? Is it about making a contribution to society? Is it about world peace? Is it about being popular?

We spend most of our lives working furiously toward goals that, when achieved, turn out to hold less substance than a doughnut.

When it comes to the pursuit of happiness, the grass is always greener on the other side of the fence. That is, we aren't happy with what we have now, but we think we just need one more thing to be happy. So we obsess over fence hopping. We get makeovers and start new adventures and change things about ourselves and become fans of Facebook causes because we know that happiness is just over the next fence.

The Bible has a lot to say about the meaning of life, actually. That makes sense since God invented life and wrote the Bible. As you can probably guess, running around like crazy trying to be happy is *not* what life is about. The meaning of life is found in God.

Life Is Short

A few years ago, right around when I was stepping into my role as lead pastor, our church was rocked by several tragedies.

First, a much-loved pastor in our church named Aaron Haskins passed away in his sleep at the age of forty-nine. Aaron was one of the most likable people I have ever known, and he had been a dear friend of my family for fifteen years. Aaron was one of those people who made everyone feel special. His death shocked us all and left a huge hole in our hearts.

My father passed away a year later, as I mentioned in the introduction. If you have lost a loved one, you understand just how hard it is. Dad was my hero, my mentor, and my best friend. He was larger than life: a man of unbelievable love, faith, and generosity. Now he was gone; our church was without its pastor, and I was without my dad.

Shortly after that, Aaron Haskins's son and namesake, Aaron Haskins Jr., died suddenly in his sleep from heart failure. He was twenty-nine. Aaron had been my friend since childhood. Now his mother, Cheryl, was dealing with the loss of her husband and her son within eighteen months. Cheryl is my hero, by the way; her strength and wisdom in that impossible season were amazing.

Our church went through a number of other difficult circumstances in that period of time. I won't list all the tragedies, but we felt them all, and it was a struggle at times just to keep going.

All of us were forced to consider how short this life is. It is a puff of smoke: here and gone in a brief flash of time. I know it doesn't feel that way when you're young, but trust me—it is.

Was life about health? About family? We had prayed long and hard for my dad's healing, then he passed away. Was the point of religion just getting God to do what we wanted? Or could we find a way to grieve our losses without being shipwrecked in our faith?

Where is the meaning in your life? So you get the honor roll. You get voted most popular. You get that amazing gaming system you've been waiting for. You get the puppy or the pony or the pet alligator. Your parents agree to take you to Hawaii over vacation.

Is that really all there is to life?

Happiness Fail

Possibly the strangest book in the Bible—certainly the most depressing—is the book of Ecclesiastes. It was written by

Solomon, a king of Israel and the wisest man who ever lived. God allowed Solomon to have everything a person might want: bottomless riches, worldwide fame, total power over a nation, popularity with the ladies, and the wisdom to manage it all.

Solomon had all the gold, glory, and girls he could wish for. And then he writes Ecclesiastes, where he basically talks about how he can't find anything in life that makes him truly happy. As you read it, you start to wonder if his goal is to depress you. This guy would have gotten along well with Eeyore and his little black rain cloud.

And yet, this book was included in the Bible. God wanted it there. It contains truth, and we could learn from Solomon's wisdom.

Solomon was smart enough to look around and see how furiously everyone was pursuing happiness. This was several thousand years ago, but the human race hasn't changed that much. Yes, since then we've invented airplanes and toilet paper, but our hearts and minds remain the same.

So Solomon decided to conduct a massive experiment in human happiness with himself at the center of the experiment. His goal, which he lays out at the beginning of the book, was to use his unbelievable resources to achieve happiness the way everyone around him was attempting to: through power, fame, pleasure, and so on. He bought into the philosophy that you can't have too much of a good thing. If a little money, a little power, and a little success felt good, a lot of it might be the ultimate source of meaning in life.

So here's this man who had everything any man would ever want. And as you read Ecclesiastes, you think, *Dude, what's wrong with this guy? Why isn't he happier?* His book describes how he always crashes and burns no matter how he tries to be happy.

Here are the first two verses of the book: "These are the words of the Teacher, King David's son, who ruled in Jerusalem. 'Everything is meaningless,' says the Teacher, 'completely meaningless!'"

And that's the high point of the book. It pretty much goes downhill from there.

Solomon criticizes, among other things:

- intelligence (1:18)
- pleasure (2:10–11)
- wisdom (2:14–16)
- work (2:21–23)
- power (4:13–16)
- righteousness (8:14)
- talent (9:11)
- education (12:12)

Confessions of a Hamster

Solomon, the wisest man who ever lived, sums up the results of his experiment at the end of his book: "Let us hear the conclusion of the whole matter: Fear God and keep His commandments, for this is man's all" (12:13 NKVJ).

I'm pretty sure that none of us will have the total wealth and power that Solomon could have used in his attempt to be happy.

But we keep trying.

Have you ever watched hamsters run around on a hamster wheel? It's funny but frustrating because they run their little hearts out and never get anywhere. And they always have this determined, desperate look on their faces like maybe *this* time the wheel will actually take them somewhere.

It's a lot like our crazy pursuit of happiness. Run like crazy . . . but never catch anything.

> Make GOD your focus, and you'll NEVER have to worry about being HAPPY.

At some point, we need to exit the hamster wheel and take an honest look at our lives. If we are not happy with the things we have now, we will never be happy. New clothes and gadgets and friends and beach vacations cannot change an unhappy person into a happy person.

That's not to say the good things of life can't bring temporary happiness. Of course they can. Money can buy happiness—it's fun to buy new things. It just isn't the kind of happiness that lasts. Then we have to buy more things, or we are left feeling emptier than ever.

Ironically, the meaning of life is not found in this life. When Solomon said, "Fear God and keep his commandments," he was saying that life is not about being happy. It's about God. Focusing on God brings meaning and joy to our lives.

Here's the crazy truth: if your life is all about making yourself happy, you won't be happy. But if your life is about loving God and loving other people, you'll end up happy. God makes life work right. He makes things make sense. Make God your focus, and you'll never have to worry about being happy. God will give you an amazing, satisfying, fun life.

Fear does not mean terror. It means total awe. We should live in an attitude of awe at the magnificence, the beauty, and the majesty of the Creator of the universe. And in that attitude, we walk with him, we trust him, and we respond in love to him.

It's interesting that fearing God comes before keeping his commandments. People who simply follow a list of laws are not in awe of God. They are bound by rules and regulations and duty. But when they fall in love with the awesomeness of God, and when they see his glory and his goodness, rules become secondary.

For many of us, that's a little confusing. Where is God? How do I see God? How can I be in awe of God?

Top Ways You Can See and Know God

1. His creation: from kittens to volcanoes to giant galaxies, the universe shows how big God is.
2. The Bible: it's a love letter from God and an instruction book for life.
3. Other people: God sends family, friends, and others to protect and guide us.
4. Circumstances: God takes care of us even when life gets crazy.
5. Jesus: Jesus is God with skin on; he shows us how much God loves us.

God is not untouchable or someone you can't know. God reveals himself in Jesus. Jesus is the awesomeness of God, the glory of God, and the ultimate picture of God. He is God with skin on.

When we are in awe of Jesus, when we recognize that he's in charge of it all, we discover the meaning of life.

Jesus is GOD with skin on.

Some of us consider ourselves followers of Jesus, but we are confused because of one thing: we are not looking to Jesus as the meaning in life.

When you are in awe of Jesus, it's amazing how uncomplicated life can be. It's amazing how uncomplicated doing the things you have to do day to day can be.

Life makes more sense when we don't make it about ourselves.

We often get distracted and bothered by little things. They don't feel little, of course—they feel like matters of life and death. Maybe you find yourself competing with the star of your soccer team. He's not a nice person, and he's not even that great of a player, but he is the team captain. That bothers you.

And all of a sudden the meaning of life is about being better than him. It's about showing that you are more athletic, more mature, and more popular than he is. You deserve to be the captain, not him. And you get worried and frustrated, and before you know it, you've lost the point of life. You think the point is proving that this kid is not who everyone thinks he is, that it's about getting the recognition you deserve.

Life makes more SENSE when we don't make it ABOUT ourselves.

So, finally, you prove you are better.

You become captain. You get the fame and glory. You are twice as popular as he ever was. But you will still find something in life to be upset about. Now, instead of the kid, it's the coach you don't like. And the cycle continues.

If we really want to find what matters in this life, we need to think about eternity. What matters most is what matters in eternity. And what matters in eternity is not income, or friendship, or fame, or fun. Those things are fine in themselves. God created them, and he loves to bless you with them. But they will not outlast death.

> What **MATTERS** most **IS** what matters in **ETERNITY.**

I love my wife. I love my kids. I like my truck and my clothes and my home. But I cannot guarantee that they will be with me forever. Life is unpredictable and short. Time and life and chance have a way of messing with our plans. Solomon proved that once and for all.

You can take my stuff. You can take my job and reputation. You can even take my family. But you cannot take Jesus away from me. He is in my heart. His awesomeness, his majesty, his generosity, his love for me—those things will last for eternity. He is the ultimate meaning in this life and the life to come in heaven.

Focal Point

I enjoy decorating my house. I don't mean the do-it-yourself kind of decorating where you build things and have to use saws and drills. Power tools and I have an agreement. I don't bother them and they don't bother me. When it comes to decorating, I like the buy-it-yourself kind, where you go to the store and *buy* furniture and artwork.

In decorating a room, there is a concept sometimes called the *focal point*. Every room has a focal point. It might be a lamp, or a wall, or a corner that everything else points to. When people walk into the room, they are drawn to that focal point. It's the first thing they notice, and it's what they remember the most.

Often, by default, the focal point is the television. Other times it's a painting. Or it's the view out a window. Or it's a giant stuffed elk head with beady glass eyes and huge antlers that your great-uncle shot with a bow and arrow on a ten-day trek through the wilderness. Hey, that's not my thing, but I live in the Northwest, and you see stuff like that.

Here's my question: What is the focal point of our lives? Is it self? Is it our efforts? Is it our good deeds? Or is it Jesus?

If Jesus is the focal point of our lives, we don't live based on what is on the earth: what we can see, touch, feel, and sense. We don't have to value what the world around us thinks is so important. Instead, we design our lives around God's truths and values.

I don't pretend to be an expert in the way other people think and feel. But I am a feelings guy, and when my emotions are out of whack, I know it—and, unfortunately, so does everyone else. I've discovered when that happens, it's usually because I've forgotten what is important. I've lost sight of Jesus. I've let the pressures and disappointments of life hijack my thoughts.

Some of us sing songs every Sunday about how good and powerful God is. We tell him we surrender our lives to him.

Then we go to school (or work, in my case) on Monday and strive and stress as if it all depended on us. We make life about ourselves: about pleasing ourselves, about accomplishing our goals, about making things happen on our own. It's a sneaky, unspoken switch that flips in our minds from Sunday to Monday, but the results are obvious: worry, sadness, fear, anxiety, pride, anger, impatience, jealousy, bitterness, gossip, confusion, and tension.

I don't know about you, but I prefer rest, peace, joy, and a feeling of purpose. That's a list I can get excited about. Once Jesus is the focal point—once he is the reason we live—everything else makes sense. Life becomes simple. Priorities fall into place, and peace, joy, and rest return.

"Come to me," Jesus calls to us today. "Come to me, all you who are weary and carry heavy burdens, and I will give you rest."

Jesus is the point of life.

Talk About It

1. Think about Solomon's downer of a book and the things that didn't make him happy. Has something you really wanted ever disappointed you? How is this like living without Jesus as your focus?
2. We talked about how God wants us to be in awe of him. What does that mean? How can you be in awe of God more?
3. What are some things the people around you are desperate for, that they think will make them happy? Will those things make them happy?

Jesus Is  HAPPY.

TEN

Real Happiness

Some people can't understand how God and happiness could go together. They think religion and fun are complete opposites. To them, God is a cosmic party pooper. A grinch. A fun sponge. A spoilsport. God is against parties and fun and pleasure, so God is the death of happiness.

Nothing could be further from the truth. God invented happiness. He came up with the concept of humor. He created our ability to have fun. He built a beautiful world and gave us five senses to enjoy it. Our pleasure gives him pleasure.

Jesus is happy. I don't know what's wrong with many of the paintings and movies about Jesus, but for some reason he looks like a zombie half the time. His eyes are freaky and he never smiles. He looks stressed out or something.

That wasn't Jesus. Do you know how I know? Because little kids liked to be with him. Small children don't like creepy people. They don't like grumpy people. Yet Jesus had so many kids wanting to come to him that his disciples almost had to put up a fence.

The Bible says about Jesus, "You love justice and hate evil. Therefore, O God, your God has anointed you, pouring out the oil of joy on you more than on anyone else" (Hebrews 1:9). The phrase "oil of joy" is a poetic way of saying that Jesus was the happiest guy around. He told jokes. He poked fun at people. He laughed.

> **JESUS was the HAPPIEST guy around.**

For some people, the thought of Jesus laughing seems out of place, like happiness means he wasn't holy or something. There is a statement I've heard that I disagree with: "God is more concerned with our holiness than our happiness." I think holiness is the key to happiness, and I think happiness can be the best expression of holiness. Really, you can't separate the two.

The Bible is full of words like *joy, rejoice, blessing, happiness,* and *peace.* Happiness is a natural result of knowing God and experiencing his love. Time and time again, when the Bible describes what it means to be a true follower of God, it uses the word *blessed.* That word means "happy" or "pleased." Real faith produces happiness, pleasure, enjoyment, and blessing.

Ways to Make People Laugh

- Wear all your clothes backward.
- Push an egg down your school hallway with your nose.

- Stuff five large marshmallows in your mouth and sing the national anthem.
- Put a carrot in your ear, and when people try to tell you that you have a carrot in your ear, yell, "What? I can't hear you—I have a carrot in my ear."
- Talk backward.
- Stare at someone silently until they stare back. Then shout, "Boo!" and walk away.
- Wrap yourself in bubble wrap—except your head, of course—and run into walls.
- Blow up a balloon and let it go. Then try to karate kick it in the air.
- Bodily functions. Need I say more?
- Just laugh—it's contagious!

Happy Feet

There is a poetic passage in Isaiah 52:7 that says, "How beautiful on the mountains are the feet of the messenger who brings good news, the good news of peace and salvation, the news that the God of Israel reigns!" This verse talks about how wonderful it is to be the person who carries good news to people who need to hear it. Messengers with good news have beautiful feet. They have happy feet.

Our good news is the fact that Jesus loves us all. It's the best news of all.

Since I'm a pastor, I'm going to pick on my own species for a minute. I was studying Luke 2 in preparation for a Christmas message a couple of years ago, and I read what the angels told the shepherds right after Jesus was born: "Don't be afraid! I bring you good news that will bring great joy to all people" (v. 10). Suddenly it hit me: my primary purpose as a preacher is to declare good news, news that produces great joy in people.

It was a wake-up call. Not that I would stand in the pulpit and scream at people before that—I'm a nice guy—but I think I was afraid of preaching too good of a gospel.

Sometimes preachers feel that we have to balance the good news and the bad news. We try to offset the really good passages with something more serious.

Understanding that the gospel is good news should help us all be a little more cheerful, a little nicer to hang out with.

> **CHURCH** is where real **PEOPLE** with real **PROBLEMS** can come and find **HOPE** and joy.

We get to share good news with people. How awesome is that? Some of us are passionate about telling people about Jesus, but we freak them out because we never learned how to smile. We wonder why they don't want anything to do with our gospel. If you say you tell people about the gospel but there is no great joy, I'd say there is a problem.

I don't want to be a person who cares more about whether a guy smokes or skips school than whether he feels loved. I don't want to be a pastor who preaches love and acceptance but avoids the teenage gang member who hangs around outside the church. I don't want to belong to a church that treats people differently because of the way they look or dress. None of this changes how God feels about them—why should it affect me?

I'm not saying it's okay to be sloppy or sketchy in church, but I am promoting a church that reflects real life, a church where real people with real problems can come and find hope and joy.

I want people in my church to welcome everybody: the good, the bad, and the ugly. I want my church to be a place where people with all kinds of backgrounds and issues and shortcomings can belong, and we don't have to get them all fixed up before they sit on the front row.

> JESUS is really good at saving PEOPLE. I'm not. I'm going to just make SURE my friend KNOWS he belongs.

That's the gospel. It's good news for everyone. It's not good news just for people who are already good, for those who are self-controlled and disciplined enough to have all their ducks in a row. It's good news for the people who can't even find their ducks. They haven't seen some of their ducks in years. Their lives are a mess. But they can come to Jesus and find instant acceptance. They belong long before they believe and long before they behave.

"Man, I don't belong here."

"Sure you do."

"No, look, everyone's dressed up all nice."

"That's just how they feel comfortable. They won't care how you dress. They won't even notice."

"I need to go out for a smoke."

"No problem, I'll save your seat."

For some of us, there's a little voice inside us asking, *So, when are you going to tell your friend about Jesus? He needs to get saved!*

Here's a tip. Jesus is really good at saving people. I'm not. So I'm going to let him do that, if you don't mind. I'm going to just make sure my friend knows he belongs.

Don't get me wrong. I'm not saying that we should never tell people about Jesus. Actually, I'm convinced that when we see how good God is, we won't be able to keep our mouths shut. We will tell them about Jesus because he has changed our lives. We will tell them about Jesus out of real love and compassion, because we know that without Jesus we would be in the same boat, and we want them to have the happiness we have found.

Dude, It's a Joke

It's not just preachers who focus on bad news more than good news. Turn on the local news; bad news abounds in our culture and society. When it comes to life in general, we are used to bad news. We are comfortable with bad news. Many of us expect bad news. I've met sickos who seem to enjoy bad news. If your joy level is low, ask yourself what kind of news you are listening to.

God is different from us. God brings good news. The angel's announcement to those shepherds when Jesus was born was the greatest good news this planet had ever heard. The shepherds figured that out. That's why they were pumped out of their minds.

It's human nature to mistrust what seems too good to be true. Let's settle in our hearts once and for all that Jesus is too good to be true. Salvation is too good to be true. Grace is too good to be true. Heaven is too good to be true.

One of the most common accusations against Christians is

not that we avoid sin; it's that we don't know how to have fun. It's our lack of joy. That's crazy. We have the best news on the planet. We know the God who created humor. Something is wrong when we call ourselves Christians but practically pull a muscle just trying to smile.

Why do people think we don't have any fun? Maybe it's because we take ourselves and our sins too seriously.

Some people take everything too seriously. They take their hair too seriously. They take flossing too seriously. They take other people's mistakes too seriously. They take their schoolwork too seriously.

More Lame Jokes

- Why did the seagull fly over the sea? Because if it flew over the bay it'd be a bagel.
- Why do gorillas have big nostrils? Because they have big fingers.
- What do you call a fish with no eye? Fssshhhh.
- Why did the scarecrow win an award? Because he was outstanding in his field.
- Which side of a zebra has the most stripes? The outside.
- What do you call cheese that isn't yours? Nacho cheese.

They even take jokes too seriously. Have you ever had someone tell you a joke and they're like, "Oh, I . . . I can't . . . that's not . . . I messed up the punch line. I just totally ruined that. I'm terrible at jokes. Why do I do this? Oh man. What's my problem? I'm just—I just totally ruined the joke. I'm sorry."

Dude, it's a joke! Don't take it so seriously.

Some people take their past too seriously. They take their present too seriously. They take their future too seriously.

We can get too serious about life, and it actually contradicts the gospel, because the gospel, by definition, is good news. There's nothing bad or sad about God's gospel. It is only good news.

Think about it. If I preached about love, joy, and happiness in my church but my kids always walked around sad and dejected, never looking people in the eyes, never talking to anyone—at some point, people would wonder what was wrong with me. My kids' attitudes are a result of who I am as a parent.

There are people who think walking around with sad looks on their faces while listing off all their problems and sacrifices makes them more spiritual, but it doesn't. It just makes them awkward to be around. It certainly doesn't make people want to hear what they have to say about God.

But the good news about Jesus produces joy in the hearts of people. It replaces depression, loneliness, and hopelessness with joy, faith, and hope.

"I bring you good news that will bring great joy to all people." That's the gospel. Joy is central. Joy is essential.

Joy of the Lord

I'm not saying you should fake joy, the smile-for-the-camera kind of joy that doesn't get into your heart. It's not about forcing laughter and bubbly words just so you'll look spiritual.

"Well, I read this book that says I have to be joyful. Because, you know, joy is part of the gospel. And I want to look like someone who believes the gospel, and if I don't smile a lot, it makes God look bad." So we laugh and smile and high-five everyone, but at home we're grouchier than ogres.

The joy of the Lord is real. It happens by itself. It leaks into the core of who we are and fills us with peace and happiness. The Bible says in Nehemiah 8:10, "Don't be dejected and sad, for the joy of the LORD is your strength!" The joy of the Lord strengthens us, calms us, and carries us. So even when life rocks our emotions for a time, we are able to strengthen ourselves by trusting in the Lord.

The gospel and joy are a package deal. It's the original Happy Meal. The box reads, "Free joy inside. No assembly required."

It's God's grace, God's joy, and God's strength, and we have free and complete access. It doesn't get better than that.

Talk About It

1. Jesus clearly liked to have fun. What do you think makes Jesus laugh (in a good way) about you and your friends?
2. Have you ever thought, *If such and such happens, then I'll be happy*? What did you think you needed to be happy?
3. How does the good news and joy of the Lord make people happy?

ELEVEN

You Belong Here

If you've ever played mini-golf or regular golf, you know how frustrating the game can be. The concept is simple: knock a little white ball into a little round hole. But it is so much harder than it sounds.

When I'm playing well, I love golf. It's my favorite sport. But when I'm not doing so well, I hate it. I have to admit, I've gotten so mad at myself a few times that I've launched clubs into the air, into trees, and even into lakes. God is still working on my patience apparently.

One of my friends is a golfer by the name of Bubba Watson. Bubba has won the biggest tournament in golf, the Master's Tournament, two times. We've played quite a few times together, and he destroys me every time. Yet I keep coming back for more. What is wrong with me?

When we've played together, Bubba or I have often brought

friends along. As you can imagine, many of them get incredibly nervous. I get a kick out of watching it. I'm warped like that.

The big reason they get nervous is they feel like they need to impress Bubba with their golf game. That, of course, is ridiculous. Whatever you can do on the golf course, I guarantee Bubba can do it better.

I tell my friends to relax. You can't impress Bubba with your golf skills. It's not going to happen. And by the way, Bubba is not criticizing your golf game. He's a nicer man than that. So just have fun. Enjoy the game. Get the most out of the experience. Laugh at your mistakes because they don't matter.

I've noticed I sometimes try to impress God. That's funny, because my goodness is even more ridiculous than my golf game.

> When GOD looks at you, he SEES his Son. That's when he says, "WOW!"

Do we think we can impress God with our love, our righteous acts, our amazing sacrifices? Is God going to leap to his feet in heaven and say, "Oh my goodness, angels, did you see that? Did someone get that on camera? Not even my Son can do that! Wow!"

We spend so much time trying to pay God back, to impress him. "See, God, see? See what I did? Do you love me more now? Will you answer more of my prayers now?"

News flash—whatever you can do, Jesus can do it better.

There is only one person God is impressed with, and that is Jesus. If you want to impress God, trust in Jesus. When you trust in Jesus, your life is wrapped up in Jesus. When God looks at you, he sees his Son. That's when he says, "Wow!"

God is not criticizing our performance. He is not judging our behavior. He is not keeping track of our sins for future reference. That was all done away with when we put our faith in Jesus. That's good news, because now we can enjoy life. Jesus did—and he was happy. Sure, there were moments when he was sad, but even in his sadness he had an unshakeable confidence in the love of the Father.

You Already Belong

One of the reasons the gospel is so good is that it's more about God than about us. That's good news, because God is a lot more trustworthy than we are.

Part of our problem is that we think about ourselves way too much. The more we obsess about our problems and our weaknesses, the more they affect us. It's weird but true.

The gospel is not about us reaching God. It's not a list of seventeen things we have to do to come close to God.

The gospel is about God coming close to us. That's why it's really good news. The amazing thing is that when we focus on his goodness, his power, and his grace, those seventeen things start to happen in our lives, all on their own. We are hardly even aware of what is happening, but the results are obvious. We begin to change; we begin to be more like Jesus.

The gospel is the opposite of religion, at least religion as many people live it. Religion says that when we obey, God accepts us. The gospel teaches the opposite: first God accepts us; then we learn to obey. Here's a little visual for you.

RELIGION: Behave ⇨ Believe ⇨ Belong
THE GOSPEL: Belong ⇨ Believe ⇨ Behave

Religion says, "Behave, believe, and then you will belong." That's the order many of us have known our whole lives. "First I have to act right, think right, and talk right, then I'll fit in. Then I'll belong."

The gospel says the opposite: "Belong, then believe, then behave." First, you *belong* to God because he created you and loves you. Second, once you get to know him, you *believe* him. Finally, after you know him, you'll naturally want to *behave,* or obey him.

Ephesians 2:8–10 says, "For by grace you have been saved through faith, and that not of yourselves; it is the gift of God, not of works, lest anyone should boast. For we are His workmanship, created in Christ Jesus for good works, which God prepared beforehand that we should walk in them" (NKJV).

Notice the divine order. First comes grace, then comes faith or belief, then comes good works. Many of us get that switched up in our minds. We think our good works come first. We have to impress God so he will accept us. We have to deserve God. So we obsess over our achievements and our holiness and our goodness. And we think, *Great joy? About what? The gospel is just a lot of work.*

God doesn't want us to make life about our clumsy efforts at holiness. He wants us to enjoy life. We only get one, after all. Sin tried to ruin it and the devil tried to steal it, but God decided to come down, in his own power, motivated by his own love, and he saved us. That's good news! If that doesn't get you excited, you better start shopping for a coffin, because you might be dead.

Happy and Holy

All of this is not to say we should continue in sin. Why would we even want to? Why would we intentionally disappoint the one who loves us the most? How ridiculous would it be to sin on purpose, knowing that sin cost Jesus his life, that it brings pain and death, and that it will mess up the happy, blessed life God created for us?

God's commandments are all motivated by his desire for our happiness, by his desire to protect us and bless us. Even his corrections are proof of his love.

When we follow the true gospel, God's commands and restrictions bring joy to our hearts. They show us the path of life. They teach us to avoid traps. They give us wisdom.

When we stop trying to impress God and instead trust in Jesus' salvation, we are free to live a new kind of holiness. It's a holiness that comes from the inside, a holiness powered by love, not by guilt. "Loving God means keeping his commandments, and his commandments are not burdensome," the apostle John wrote. "For every child of God defeats this evil world, and we achieve this victory through our faith" (1 John 5:3–4). It's incredible, really—when we let Jesus love us and learn to love him in return, holiness just happens.

I think there should be no such thing as a *grouchy Christian*. As I said earlier, holiness turns into happiness, and happiness is an expression of

> When we let **JESUS** love us and learn to **LOVE** him in return, holiness just **HAPPENS.**

holiness. The two go together. I am happier because I am holy, and it's easier to be holier because I am happy. Because of the good news, because of Jesus, I can be both holy and happy—what a concept!

Are You Talking to Us?

The gospel is good news because it can be summed up in the phrase "God with us." Matthew 1:23 quotes a passage from the Old Testament that predicts Jesus' birth: "Look! The virgin will conceive a child! She will give birth to a son, and they will call him Immanuel, which means 'God is with us.'"

That is the gospel: God is with us. Jesus was God in the flesh, here on earth, hanging out with sinful people. That isn't just good news. It's great news. It's crazy, amazing, mind-blowing news.

It's fascinating that the first people who hear about Jesus' birth are shepherds. Because of the nature of their job, shepherds were unable to fulfill parts of the religious ceremonial law, including the frequent hand washings. Shepherds were actually despised by the religious people of the day because they could never completely fulfill the law.

The angel came to those who couldn't fulfill the law and told them that someone has come who will fulfill the law for them.

"Us? Are you talking to us?" the shepherds must have asked the angel.

"Yeah, to you, you lawbreakers. This child is born for you. He is a gift to you. He is for you. He is with you."

Things That Made the Shepherds Not So Popular

- They didn't take a lot of showers.
- They had sheep doo on their sandals.
- Their conversation mostly had to do with sheep ("Uh, hey—who's your favorite sheep?").
- They were too busy scaring away wolves and bears to go to parties.

No wonder these shepherds were so excited. They were thinking, *Is this a mistake? I bet they meant to go to the house of one of the rabbis. Maybe their GPS malfunctioned or something. We don't even keep the law—why are they coming to us?*

To truly understand this phrase "God is with us," you have to know that they lived in a time period when you couldn't access God that easily. But now, suddenly, he was among them. A holy, righteous, perfect, just God had come down to live with sinners, with people who could not fulfill the law. They could see him, they could hear him, they could touch him. He was with them.

Jesus is in heaven now, but his life, death, and resurrection changed everything. Now we don't live under the law, which kept God and man separate. The new relationship to God that Jesus gave us says that God will always be with us. It's his promise to mankind. He is always available to us.

That's the good news of the gospel.

> It's his **PROMISE** to mankind. He is **ALWAYS** available to us.

Talk About It

1. Have you ever moved to a new neighborhood or school and felt like you didn't belong? How did that feel? How does it feel to know that you already belong with God?
2. What would you do in life if you knew you'd always belong and be accepted? How would your everyday life change?
3. What did it mean that the announcement of Jesus came to the shepherds, who were misfits in their culture? Why was that good news for them?

Jesus Is HERE.

TWELVE

The One You Love

I have a big mouth. Literally, I do. I remember playing with my cousins once when we were kids, and someone had the great idea of holding a vote on who had the biggest facial features. If I remember right, I won in every category except biggest ears. I don't think it was a compliment. I clearly remember that when it came to mouths, it was unanimous: I had the biggest mouth.

I also happen to have a big mouth when it comes to talking. I like to talk. A lot. Probably too much, now that I think about it. I can't tell you how many times I've gotten myself into trouble by popping off with some comment without thinking. The comments are usually hilarious, if I do say so myself, but for some reason that doesn't usually help.

Maybe you've done it too. You're in the heat of the moment, and you don't mean to, but something wells up inside, and you blurt it out. These comments tend to say a lot about us, actually.

They are an unplanned, unfiltered result of what is in our minds and hearts. The Bible says that out of the abundance of the heart, the mouth speaks.

Ways to Keep from Blurting Things Out

1. Duct tape.
2. Hold your breath and count to ten million.
3. Say what you wanted to say but in an English accent (unless you're English, in which case use an American accent). I promise you won't be able to stay mad.
4. Say what you wanted to say but with your mouth closed.
5. Do jumping jacks while singing, "Mommy made me eat my M&M's" as loudly as you can.
6. Pray.
7. Lock yourself in the restroom until you cool down. If you're in a hurry, put your head under the sink.
8. Stick a giant spoonful of peanut butter in your mouth.

When you're in the HEAT of the moment, what YOU really believe comes OUT.

When you're in the heat of the moment, typically what you really believe comes out. What you really want to say slips out, and you can't get it back. It can be painful or embarrassing, but it can also be revealing.

We can tell what we really believe about God by what comes out of our mouths in tough times. This is exactly what happened to some of Jesus' friends when they were going through a tragedy.

Jesus' Friend

In John 11, we find a moving story about three siblings who were close friends of Jesus: Martha, Mary, and Lazarus. Most scholars believe Martha was the oldest sibling, Mary was the middle, and Lazarus was the little brother. Interestingly, Lazarus was never recorded as saying one word in Scripture. Apparently his big sisters said it all. Poor guy.

In this passage, Mary and Martha are in the heat of the moment. Their little brother's life is on the line. The Bible puts it this way:

> Now, a certain man was sick, Lazarus of Bethany, the town of Mary and her sister Martha. It was that Mary who anointed the Lord with fragrant oil and wiped His feet with her hair, whose brother Lazarus was sick. Therefore, the sisters sent to Him saying, "Lord, behold, he whom You love is sick."
>
> When Jesus heard that, He said, "This sickness is not unto death, but for the glory of God, that the Son of God may be glorified through it."
>
> Now, Jesus loved Martha and her sister and Lazarus. (John 11:1–5 NKJV)

Besides his disciples, Martha, Mary, and Lazarus were perhaps Jesus' best friends. Jesus loved them deeply.

The fact that Jesus had friends at all might surprise a few people who think he floated around two feet off the ground and only had time for healing people and preaching. He was a normal-looking and normal-acting guy. Except he healed the sick, raised the dead, and never sinned. And he was God. No biggie.

In this story, Lazarus is hours from death. He is on the door-step of death. And Mary and Martha, as usual, are speaking on Lazarus's behalf. They need to get God's attention. They have one shot at convincing Jesus to come. They need to come up with their best argument. So they write Jesus a note. It has to be a good one—their brother's life depends on it.

It's the heat of the moment, and they aren't thinking about being polite and using the most beautiful words. What they really believe is about to be revealed. What are they going to write to Jesus? What will their plea be?

Now, if we were Lazarus's siblings, a lot of us would have started out by listing all the good things Lazarus had done. We would have talked about how much he loved and admired Jesus and how he was a model citizen who didn't deserve to die.

Not Mary and Martha.

They knew what moved Jesus.

"Lord, the one that *you love* is sick."

> "LORD, the one that you LOVE is sick."

That was the truth that came up from deep within their hearts. Jesus loved Lazarus, and that was what mattered most.

Notice it wasn't their love for Jesus, or Lazarus's love for God, or Lazarus's good deeds that moved Jesus. It was pointless to recite a list of their brother's achievements. That wasn't what moved the heart of Jesus. It was his own love that motivated him. It was his own desire to bless and heal and restore.

The story goes on to say that Jesus responded to Mary and Martha's request and went to their home. But by the time he arrived, Lazarus had died. That didn't scare Jesus—he already knew that was going to happen. He simply raised Lazarus from the dead. It pays to have friends like that.

John, one of Jesus' disciples, wrote down this story. John understood the importance of Jesus' love. Five times in his book, John calls himself "the disciple whom Jesus loved." He doesn't even use his own name. He just flaunts that he was Jesus' favorite.

Was he Jesus' favorite? We don't know. It doesn't really matter, because he believed he was. And there is something very healthy about that perspective. We are all God's favorite.

Some might call John's statements arrogant, but John didn't care. Neither did God, apparently—it's in his book. John described himself using Jesus' love. In other words, the most important thing in John's life and the thing that best described him wasn't what he did, what his grade average was, or where he lived. It was the fact that Jesus loved him. I find that fascinating.

WE are all God's FAVORITES.

A few decades later, John wrote several letters that are also part of the Bible. The letters are a description of God's love toward us. Here's one example from 1 John 4:9–10:

> God showed how much he loved us by sending his one and only Son into the world so that we might have eternal life through him. This is real love—not that we loved God, but that he loved us and sent his Son as a sacrifice to take away our sins.

John figured something out by watching Jesus. It's not about how much we love God. It's about how much he loves us.

Let Me Count the Ways

Let's go back to the story of Lazarus. The message Mary and Martha sent was a plea, a prayer. And notice the basis of their prayer: "the one you love."

You can find out a lot about what you really believe when you listen to yourself pray, when you listen to what you say in the heat of the moment. How many times have I prayed prayers like this: "Oh, God, I need help. I'm faithful. I help people. I'm generous. I'm holy. I read my Bible. And I'm praying really, really loudly, with Bible verses and lots of compliments and promises. So come, Lord, and help me with my need."

In other words, "Lord, based on what I've done, now please do . . ." We think that moves God. No, what moves God is his Son. What moves God is his love.

One of the most famous love poems of all time is Sonnet 43 by Elizabeth Barrett Browning. If you haven't read it yet, you will—in a class on English literature. It starts out, "How do I love thee? Let me count the ways."

Don't count the ways you love God; count the ways he loves you. Your love is tiny compared to his. So when you pray, pray like Mary and Martha: "Jesus, the one you love needs you."

I was tired the other afternoon, for instance. Maybe not a big deal, but I had some things I had to accomplish that evening, and I really needed strength. So I got alone for a few minutes, and I said, "Lord, the one you love is tired. Give me energy."

Counting the Ways God Loves You

1. He loves you forever.
2. He loves you first.
3. He loves you when you don't deserve it.
4. He loves you like a father loves a child.
5. He loves your personality, and he thinks you're awesome.
6. He loves what you love—your hopes, your dreams, your desires.
7. He loves you so much that he has great things planned for your future.
8. How else does God love you? _____

It was such a refreshing, healthy way to pray. It was incredible. I started thinking, *Whoa. That was crazy. That felt good.*

He's moved by his love. Remind yourself of that. It makes praying a lot more fun.

"Lord, the one you love forgot his lunch money. Again. But I'm your favorite. I'm the one you love, so help me with this, Lord."

That's far better than trying to talk God into something based on our own works or our own goodness.

Maybe you are thinking, *I don't really know Jesus. How can I talk to him this way?*

If you're like me, sometimes you find yourself time and time again worrying about not being enough for God, or not having enough love for him. But when you look at the Bible, you discover that it is all about God's love for *us*. In fact, God's love created our love. All sixty-six books of the Bible, all forty-plus authors writing over the course of sixteen hundred years, point to the same thing: God's love for us—for you and me.

None of us are outsiders when we pray based on *his* love, not ours. No matter who you are, no matter what you need, try praying that prayer. And I pray that your heart explodes with an understanding of his amazing love for you.

"God, because I am the focus of your heart, because I'm the one you love, come now and take care of my needs."

Here's a crazy thought: God's love is so over-the-top enormous that he loved us before we were even us. He loved us before we *existed*. He knew that many people would not care about him—would even reject him. Yet he chose to love us anyway. God loves us because he is love. John, the "one Jesus loved," spelled it out: "We love Him because He first loved us" (1 John 4:19 NKJV).

> He LOVED us before we WERE even us. He loved us before we EXISTED.

The reason we are even interested in God is that he is hot on our trails. We are his favorites, and he is passionately pursuing us. He doesn't just love us like a friend, like an aunt or uncle, or even like a dad. His love is far more perfect than any of those.

We won't totally understand it until we enter heaven and spend eternity with him. And when we get to eternity, we will be shocked. We will be overwhelmed and stunned and amazed by the hugeness of his love.

Picture that the next time you pray, the next time you fail at something, or the next time you are facing a tough situation—it will change everything.

Go ahead and try to describe the height of his love, the

length of his love, the width of his love, the depth of his love. Our comparisons can't come close. We might have parents, we might have siblings and family, we might have friends, but nothing compares to God's love for us.

I've never met a person who overestimated God's love. Never. It's impossible. He loved us first, he loves us best, and he will love us forever.

How does he love me?

I'll spend the rest of my life counting the ways.

Talk About It

1. Make a list of a few prayer requests or things you need help with, and start to pray, "Lord, the one you love is (fill in the blank). Help me (fill in the blank)."

2. Why wasn't it weird for John to call himself Jesus' favorite?

3. You have ten seconds: describe God. Go!

4. What did your answers to the last question show you about who God is to you?

THIRTEEN

With Us and for Us

People's last words are usually pretty meaningful. Whether they are leaving for a long journey or they are on their deathbed, they use their last few moments to say what is most important to them.

The last few chapters of Matthew describe Jesus' crucifixion and resurrection, which I'll talk about again later. Matthew 28 gives us some of Jesus' last words on earth. Jesus is about to leave his disciples and return to heaven. The disciples are pumped that Jesus is alive, but now he is leaving again.

Knowing he will not see them again in this life, Jesus leaves them with several important thoughts. He isn't just talking to them, of course—he is talking to us. His last few words to his followers are as true today as they were two thousand years ago.

Of all the things Jesus probably said that day, Matthew, the tax-collector-turned-disciple, chose to finish his book with these words: "And be sure of this: I am with you always, even to the end of the age." Clearly, this promise meant a lot to him.

With You Always

I'm sure Matthew was heartbroken at the thought of losing Jesus, especially after the roller-coaster emotions of seeing him crucified and then seeing him alive again. Jesus had completely changed Matthew's life. Because Jesus had believed in him, because Jesus took time for him, Matthew had gone from being a guy with a terrible reputation to being one of Jesus' twelve disciples. Now Jesus was leaving the earth physically, but he promised to always be there for them—to be here for us.

> "I am WITH you always, even to the END of the age."

What does that mean? We can't see him. We can't hear him. We can't talk with him or hug him or laugh with him, at least not in person, like we can with our friends and family. When Jesus said he would be with his disciples, he wasn't talking about being present in a human body. That would be impossible, because even though he was God, he had taken on human form and could only be in one place at a time. No, he was talking about something better.

Long before Jesus was crucified, he told his disciples that one day he would be killed, but he would return from the dead and then go back up to heaven. They couldn't believe it. They even got on his case for being so negative. But he promised them it was actually better that way. He said God would send the Holy Spirit, who would be a comforter, counselor, and teacher.

God actually shows himself to us in three different ways: the Father, the Son (Jesus), and the Holy Spirit. That doesn't mean there are three Gods—there is only one. However, the three parts or persons of God are different.

Confused? That's okay. God has it figured out. He's not having an identity crisis because we don't understand him completely. As humans, we can only understand so much, so we have a tough time understanding an infinite being. Actually, it's not just tough—it's impossible. If we could understand him, he wouldn't be God.

What is important is that we realize that Jesus—who is God—went back to heaven, but he didn't leave us alone. He sent the Holy Spirit—who is God—in his place. It's actually better for us because the Holy Spirit can be everywhere at once.

Jesus brought the presence of God to us permanently. We don't have to beg God to come to us. We don't have to plead with him to pay attention to us. He is with us all the time.

Jesus Is with You . . .

- when you're taking that super hard science test.
- while you're hanging out with your friends.
- when your parents make rules you don't like.
- when you're trying to do the right thing, even if it might make you unpopular.
- when you feel alone.

- when you are happier than you've ever been before.
- when you're sadder than you've ever been before.
- when you finally land that skateboard move.
- . . . and every other time in between.

Jesus is with you in your home and at your school. He's with you when you're doing great, and he's with you in your mistakes. You'll probably go through some rough moments in life, like everyone does, and you might feel scared or upset. Always remember that God is there. His voice calms the storm and gives you rest.

Jesus isn't just with you when you are doing well, or full of faith, or living in holiness. He loved you when you hated him, and he loves you now. He is head-over-heels in love with you. He is on your side not because of who you are but because of who he is. His love is unconditional and overwhelming. He is with you, he is on your side, and he is your biggest fan.

No problem is so big, no failure so bad, and no enemy so terrible that Jesus can't give you the victory. Jesus speaks today, just as he did to his disciples so long ago.

"Be sure of this: I am with you always."

Why Are You Here?

Have you ever had somebody show up at your house unexpectedly? Maybe it's around dinnertime, and you're just getting ready to sit down and eat, and you hear the doorbell. You open it up, and it's a friend of yours.

And you're like, "Hey."

"Hey, I'm here."

"Great! Hi!" And you're frantically searching through your brain, trying to remember if you invited your friend over and just forgot or what. Finally you ask, "Uh, why? Why are you here?"

"What do you mean? I'm just here."

"You're just here? Well, my family—we're sitting down for dinner, but—"

"Cool. Cool."

"Oh, so you came to eat?"

"No, I just came to be here."

It's just awkward.

We have to ask ourselves, why is Jesus with us?

This is where it goes to the next level, and a lot of people can't take it. They can agree that God is with them, but they just don't know why.

The Bible declares that God is with us *because God is for us*. He's here to make sure we're taken care of. He's here to hook us up and back us up. He's here to provide, protect, and empower.

> **GOD is with us because God is FOR US.**

Romans 8:31–32 makes this clear: "What shall we say about such wonderful things as these? If God is for us, who can ever be against us? Since he did not spare even his own Son but gave him up for us all, won't he also give us everything else?"

Some people argue this, which is unthinkable to me. Why would you argue that God is not for you?

"Well," they say, "sometimes he comes in his anger, and he comes with punishment, and he comes—"

Hold on. You mean to tell me that you don't think God is for you, even though he gave his Son for you? He's so for you that he died for you. What other proof do you need?

My dad used to ask people, "How good does God need to be to you before you're happy?" That's not a critical statement. It's a wake-up call. We have a good God and we have a good Savior. Our lives are good. We have a lot to be grateful for and a lot to be happy about.

Some of us go so far as to think God gets a kick out of our suffering.

"Yeah, it's good for you to suffer. Learn your lesson."

That's wrong. That's bizarre. If people did that to other people, they'd be put in jail.

I love what God says through the prophet Jeremiah: "'For I know the plans I have for you,' says the LORD. 'They are plans for good and not for disaster, to give you a future and a hope.'"

> "I know your **FUTURE**, and it is full of **HOPE!**"

In other words, "Don't tell me I'm here to do you bad. Don't tell me I'm here to judge you. Don't tell me I'm here because I'm mad at you. I know the thoughts I think about you, and they're for good, not for evil. I know your future, and it is full of hope!"

God is with us, and he is for us. This is the gospel.

So no matter what I go through, he is with me and he is for me. Even if it doesn't make sense, he is with me and he is for me. Even if I can't do my best, he is with me and he is for me. No matter what anybody says, he is with me and he is for me. No matter what my emotions tell me, no matter what my pain or sickness tells me, no matter what other people tell me, he is with me and he is for me. He is on my side.

Saved Alone

I suppose some could get the wrong idea that because Jesus is with us, everything will be perfect and easy for us. Some of us might think that the difference between those who love Jesus and those who don't is that the people who love him get everything they want: nice clothes, the newest phones, friends and popularity, and good health. They will have abundant life because that's what Jesus promises.

Yes, God wants to bless you. Yes, God is for you. He's for your happiness, he's for your health, he's for your finances, and he's for your success.

But without a doubt, bad things happen to good people. Life is not always easy or pleasant. It doesn't always make sense. There are times we feel alone, abandoned, and hopeless.

When we understand that Jesus is here, though, we can make it through anything. People who know that Jesus loves them, who know that Jesus is with them and for them—those people can not only endure pain and loss and difficulty, they can come out the other side stronger and better people. They can be more alive than a person who seems to have it so easy but is apart from Jesus.

The Bible says, "Though I walk through the valley of the shadow of death, I will fear no evil; for You are with me" (Psalm 23:4 NKJV).

When we have Jesus, we have everything we will ever need

for anything we could ever go through. Maybe things aren't going smoothly for us right now. Maybe everything isn't wonderful. Maybe we are going through hurt and pain and loss.

Jesus gives us the grace to stand and say, "It is well with my soul," because he is here. In the middle of hard times, our souls can find rest and hope.

Things to Remember When You're Feeling Sad

1. You are not alone, even though it might feel like you are.
2. It is okay to be sad, to cry, and even to get mad.
3. Jesus never wants terrible things to happen to you—he only wants what's good for you.
4. God doesn't give people pain so they "get what they deserve." He cries with us.
5. Reaching out to God and other people will help. Talk about it.
6. Keep praying—never give up on talking to God.

Jesus Wept

I am not trying to act like loss isn't that bad. I am not implying that we should hide our feelings or criticize those who are sad. Far from it. The death of my father was a journey of sorrow and grief that rocked me to my core. I spent months figuring out my feelings and trying to regain my sense of myself after my father was gone.

But through the roller-coaster years of sickness, through my father's death, and through suddenly finding myself responsible for leading a church of thousands of people, I was never alone.

Jesus is alive, and Jesus is with me. He is my life, my peace, my confidence. I don't claim to have had a perfect attitude, but I found a depth of love and strength in Jesus that I had never known before.

I wish I could put into words the presence of Jesus that strengthened me, but maybe it's something you have to go through to understand. What I can tell you is that it is there when we need it. Jesus is more real, more present, more alive, and more with us than we know. Sometimes it takes tragic events for us to realize how real our faith is.

"Here on earth you will have many trials and sorrows," Jesus said. "But take heart, because I have overcome the world" (John 16:33).

The story of Lazarus's death that we talked about earlier shows Jesus' love and understanding when we go through difficult experiences. John 11:35, one of the shortest but most meaningful verses in the Bible, says, "Then Jesus wept." Jesus doesn't ignore our grief. He weeps with us.

If you read the rest of that story, you figure out Jesus knew the whole time that Lazarus would die, and Jesus knew he was going to raise him from the dead. So why weep? Why waste his tears? Why not instead tell off the people for their lack of faith or take the opportunity to point out his own power?

He wept because their grief moved him. Their sorrow brought out his compassion.

But Jesus didn't just grieve with them. He raised Lazarus from the dead, and he brings life to us too.

"I am the resurrection and the life," Jesus told Martha.

"Anyone who believes in me will live, even after dying. Everyone who lives in me and believes in me will never ever die" (John 11:25–26).

The fact that Jesus is here not only brings comfort in hard times, it gives us courage that things can change for the better. Jesus brings life out of death. He brings hope out of sorrow. He turns our mourning into joy. Jesus is there for us when we need him most—whether we know it or not and whether we appreciate it or not.

Jesus will never leave us. He will never abandon us. He will never give up on us.

Jesus is always here.

Talk About It

1. When has someone cried with you or been with you in a sad time to comfort you? Is there something right now that you're having a tough time with?
2. What are some things that might make us think Jesus isn't "for us"? How can we remember he's there in those times?
3. How do you usually react when something bad happens?
4. When was the last time something terrible happened that made you upset, like it did for Mary and Martha? Does it make a difference to think of Jesus weeping for you and with you?

Jesus Is ALIVE.

FOURTEEN

Zombie Jesus

The gospel of Matthew ends on a spectacular note. Earlier, I quoted the final verse, in which Jesus promises to be with us always. Actually, the entire final chapter is an exclamation mark celebrating the greatest victory in Jesus' life and challenging us with a glorious future.

The setting is right after Jesus' death. The Roman government was relieved because the guy who had sparked so much civil unrest was no longer their problem. The Pharisees were thrilled because their competition had been wiped out. The disciples were terrified and confused because this was not at all how they thought things would work out.

Here is chapter 28:

Early on Sunday morning, as the new day was dawning, Mary Magdalene and the other Mary went out to visit the tomb.

Suddenly there was a great earthquake! For an angel of the Lord came down from heaven, rolled aside the stone, and sat on it. His face shone like lightning, and his clothing was as white as snow. The guards shook with fear when they saw him, and they fell into a dead faint.

Then the angel spoke to the women. "Don't be afraid!" he said. "I know you are looking for Jesus, who was crucified. He isn't here! He is risen from the dead, just as he said would happen. Come, see where his body was lying. And now, go quickly and tell his disciples that he has risen from the dead, and he is going ahead of you to Galilee. You will see him there. Remember what I have told you."

The women ran quickly from the tomb. They were very frightened but also filled with great joy, and they rushed to give the disciples the angel's message. And as they went, Jesus met them and greeted them. And they ran to him, grasped his feet, and worshiped him. Then Jesus said to them, "Don't be afraid! Go tell my brothers to leave for Galilee, and they will see me there."

As the women were on their way, some of the guards went into the city and told the leading priests what had happened. A meeting with the elders was called, and they decided to give the soldiers a large bribe. They told the soldiers, "You must say, 'Jesus' disciples came during the night while we were sleeping, and they stole his body.' If the governor hears about it, we'll stand up for you so you won't get in trouble." So the guards accepted the bribe and said what they were told to say. Their story spread widely among the Jews, and they still tell it today.

Then the eleven disciples left for Galilee, going to the

mountain where Jesus had told them to go. When they saw him, they worshiped him—but some of them doubted!

Jesus came and told his disciples, "I have been given all authority in heaven and on earth. Therefore, go and make disciples of all the nations, baptizing them in the name of the Father and the Son and the Holy Spirit. Teach these new disciples to obey all the commands I have given you. And be sure of this: I am with you always, even to the end of the age."

#winning

In one moment, everything changed. This was the ultimate happy ending, the original buzzer-beater. Everyone knew Jesus was dead. They saw the Roman soldiers execute him, and Roman soldiers were professionals at killing people.

But now he's alive. He's popping up in random places, scaring the heck out of his already freaked-out disciples. He's taking selfies and posting them with the caption, "I'm back, dudes. #winning."

The Romans and the Pharisees are left scrambling, while the disciples are out of their minds with joy. A few of Jesus' followers needed some convincing because like many of us, they were more likely to believe bad news than good news.

Really? Jesus must have thought. *I come back from the dead and my friends don't even recognize me. Lame.*

But Jesus was back, just as he had promised.

And speaking of zombie apocalypses—which we weren't, but my brain works like that—you could call Jesus the ultimate zombie. He was killed, then he came back from the dead, and now he's coming for you.

Okay—some of you would do well to discover a sense of humor. You'll live longer.

Here's the deal. If Jesus' death was the end of the story, there's nothing really special about that. People die all the time—even good people. It's part of being human.

Lots of people have even given their lives for their beliefs. We remember them and call them "martyrs," and their legacies inspire us. Sometimes we get a day off in their honor, but that is about it.

If Jesus Rose from the Dead . . .

- I don't have to be afraid of sickness or death.
- I can trust God even when things seem impossible.
- I can pray big prayers because God can do anything.
- I know that sin and the devil are defeated and Jesus always wins.
- I know someday I'll be in heaven with Jesus.

But if it's true Jesus rose from the dead, then that changes everything. That means he conquered the final enemy: death. That means everything he claimed about himself is true. He isn't just human. He is God. He is the answer to mankind's problems. He is the Savior.

The Pharisees figured this out quicker than many of us. Whether they actually thought he came back to life or not, we don't know. I suspect some of them did, but they couldn't process it. They couldn't adjust their thinking. They didn't want to mess with the way things were.

They knew what would happen if rumor got out that he was back. It would change their entire way of life. The religious authorities would no longer be the way to God; Jesus would be the way to God. Sinners would no longer be kept away from God; they would be welcomed by God. People would no longer have to follow impossible laws; they would follow Jesus, whose yoke was easy and whose burden was light, and they would live in the wide-open spaces of grace.

So the Pharisees lied. And they bribed the Roman guards to spread the lie. And they promised to protect the guards whom they had bribed. Yes, it was messy, but it easier to them than accepting God's grace and his plan in Jesus, which was to die for our sins.

But Jesus didn't just die on the cross. He rose from the dead.

That's what a God would do, because an eternal, infinite God can't be killed—at least not permanently—by the people he created. The resurrection proves that everything he said was true. It gives us all hope that we can win in this life. It proves that life continues after our time on earth is over.

The gospel is good news because of the resurrection. The gospel isn't just that Jesus died for our sins. That's the first half. The second half is that Jesus rose again, proving once and for all that sin and death were beaten, and we can have eternal life.

Hollow Chocolate Bunnies

When I was growing up, my parents bought me a chocolate Easter bunny every year. And every year I would open the box, pull out the bunny, and bite off an ear, hoping that this would be the year that the bunny was actually solid chocolate. It never was. It was hollow. Every stinking year. Why was I never allowed the luxury of having a solid chocolate Easter bunny? Why?

Paul wrote in 1 Corinthians 15:16–20,

> And if there is no resurrection of the dead, then Christ has not been raised. And if Christ has not been raised, then your faith is useless and you are still guilty of your sins. In that case, all who have died believing in Christ are lost! And if our hope in Christ is only for this life, we are more to be pitied than anyone in the world.
>
> But in fact, Christ has been raised from the dead. He is the first of a great harvest of all who have died.

Paul is telling the Christians in Corinth that if Jesus was not raised from the dead, then their faith was as hollow as a chocolate Easter bunny. No substance. No meaning. No point. Just empty.

If Jesus didn't rise again, it means we are still in our sins. His death didn't work. It wasn't good enough. He wasn't strong enough to defeat the final enemy, death.

We have to understand that death was not part of God's original creation. It was an effect of sin.

He goes so far as to say that if Christianity is just about being good in this life and nothing more, then we are the most pitiful creatures on the planet.

In other words, this life is not the point.

> Death was NOT part of God's ORIGINAL creation.

This life is wonderful, and God has good things for us while we are here on earth. But Jesus didn't give his life to promote a list of dos and don'ts. He didn't suffer and die for world peace. Our faith isn't about studying the Bible, or praying, or going to church. All of those things are good, but Jesus' victory was bigger.

Jesus came so we could live forever with him. That's true life.

No Matter What, We Win

The Bible talks a lot about miracles and God healing people. In our church, we have prayed for many sick people and have seen genuine healings, even in very difficult situations. Not everyone has been healed, but many have. I am convinced of God's willingness and his power to heal the sick, just as Jesus did so many years ago.

So when my father received that terrible diagnosis of cancer, my family and our church fought the good fight of faith. We prayed continually for my dad. We trusted the teachings of the Bible and believed that God would heal his body and prolong his life.

The people in our church are amazing, let me just say that. Their love in that hard time still moves me to tears. My family will forever be in their debt. We walked through the valley of the shadow of death together, and even in the darkest of times, they did not stop having faith.

For several years my dad had almost no symptoms of cancer. The treatments had difficult side effects at times, but the cancer itself seemed to be controlled. Our faith was high. Our prayers were energetic and full of confidence.

After several more years, however, he began to worsen. He got sicker. His pain increased. The treatments were slowing the progress of the cancer, but his health had taken a definite turn for the worse.

As the situation changed, we were all forced to question what we really believed about God, about death, and about the meaning of life. I don't think we doubted God's goodness or power to heal, but we had to wrestle with questions we never thought we would face.

What if Pastor Wendell doesn't get healed? You could tell it was on everyone's mind. *For years now, we've been praying for his healing, believing for his healing, talking about how sure we are that he is going to be healed—but what if he dies? What happens to our faith then?*

> "No MATTER what happens, we WIN."

I had recently become the preaching pastor of our church. My dad was still the senior pastor, but because of his health he was rarely able to preach. So every weekend I would stand before the church and declare the goodness and power of God. And every weekend I could see the questions in people's eyes.

But my parents' faith was rock solid, and all of us took heart and grew in faith as we watched them. My dad said it best: "No matter what happens, we win."

That was what I reminded people week after week when I preached. Whether God healed him or took him home, we could not lose. If he was healed, that would be a tremendous victory.

But if not, heaven would not be defeat. It would be the greatest victory of all.

In 2010, a few days before Christmas, my dad passed away. He is in a better place—an unimaginably better place. He finished his race, he fought the good fight of faith, and he passed the baton to the next generation. Now I believe he's looking down on me and on our church, cheering us on.

Why Heaven Is Awesome

- No tests. No homework. No detention.
- Freedom from pain, sadness, and tears.
- Skateboarding on streets of gold.
- Perfect health. And probably huge muscles.
- Spending eternity with friends.
- No more temptation, sin, guilt, or punishment.
- Getting autographs from people like Noah, Jonah, David, and Mary.
- Being more alive than we ever have been.
- Getting to hug God and hear him say how much he loves us.

We were sad, of course, and the loss was so hard. We still miss him every single day. But our viewpoint in this life is based on eternity. We know we will see him again. We know that God's goodness and love and power are as real as ever.

The Bible calls death the final enemy. It's a bigger enemy than sickness, doubt, fear, sin, poverty, or pain. Jesus conquered this final enemy when he was brought back to life in the resurrection. That means we don't have to fear anything—even death. Heaven was the ultimate victory for my dad. Death did not defeat him, because Jesus had already defeated death.

Romans 5:21 says, "So just as sin ruled over all people and brought them to death, now God's wonderful grace rules instead, giving us right standing with God and resulting in eternal life through Jesus Christ our Lord." Sin, death, and the devil hold no threat when we know who we are in Jesus.

> We DON'T have to fear anything— even DEATH.

This is how we gain perspective in life. It's the gospel that brings things back into proportion. Bad news is everywhere, but the good news of the gospel beats it every time. Obstacles may tower in front of you, but Jesus is greater than them all.

Talk About It

1. If Jesus is in control and "we win" no matter what, what's the worst that can happen?
2. What is so scary about dying? Have you ever been afraid of it? How does the fact that Jesus came back from the dead affect the way you look at death?

FIFTEEN

New Way to Be Human

Admit it: at some point in your childhood, you ran around the house in a cape and/or mask, pretending to be a superhero. There's no shame in that. There is something fascinating about the idea of having superpowers, of not being limited by the same things that affect the rest of the world.

Maybe your favorite superpower was the ability to fly, or superhuman strength, or X-ray vision, or invisibility. Maybe you dreamed of saving the world—or of saving one girl in particular.

Check Off Your Three Favorite Superpowers

- ❑ Speak to animals
- ❑ Control weather
- ❑ Elasticity
  (stretchiness)

- ❑ Healing
- ❑ Invisibility
- ❑ Flight
- ❑ X-ray vision

- ❑ Mind control
- ❑ Plant control
- ❑ Super hearing
- ❑ Super strength
- ❑ Super speed
- ❑ Time travel
- ❑ Laser eyes
- ❑ Breathe underwater
- ❑ Understand all languages
- ❑ Ability to spit lava
- ❑ Produce earthquakes

What if I told you there was a way to live outside of the limits of normal human life? I can't promise you hands that shoot spider webs or eyes that blast laser beams, but I can tell you about a supernatural, superhuman power to live the best life imaginable.

Paul, one of the authors of the New Testament, describes it this way in Colossians 3:1–11:

Since you have been raised to new life with Christ, set your sights on the realities of heaven, where Christ sits in the place of honor at God's right hand. Think about the things of heaven, not the things of earth. For you died to this life, and your real life is hidden with Christ in God. And when Christ, who is your life, is revealed to the whole world, you will share in all his glory.

So put to death the sinful, earthly things lurking within you. Have nothing to do with sexual immorality, impurity, lust, and evil desires. Don't be greedy, for a greedy person is an idolater, worshiping the things of this world. Because of these sins, the anger of God is coming. You used to do these things when your life was still part of this world. But now is the time to get rid of anger, rage, malicious behavior, slander, and dirty language. Don't lie to each other, for you have stripped off your old sinful nature and all its wicked deeds. Put on your new nature, and be renewed as you learn to know your Creator and become like him. In this new life, it doesn't matter if you are a Jew or a Gentile, circumcised or uncircumcised, barbaric, uncivilized, slave, or free. Christ is all that matters, and he lives in all of us.

Jesus gives us a new way to be human.

In Jesus, and only in Jesus, we are offered a new way of living. When Jesus rose from the dead, we rose from the dead too, on a spiritual level. Someday we'll physically rise too, but for now we have a new spiritual life, a new nature.

Our "superpower" is the ability to live free from the power of sin that affects the rest of the world. We don't have to be greedy. We don't have to be controlled by anger. We don't have to give in to the wrong desires that used to affect us. We are free to live life the way God meant for us to live it.

Sit Down

In Colossians 3, Paul shows us what it looks like to live grace Monday through Saturday. Notice his opening word: "Since." It's a simple word that has massive meaning. It means, "Based on everything I'm saying, do this."

If you read back, you'll find Paul had just taken two chapters to talk about the incredible grace of God at work in our lives. He described Jesus and his work on the cross. He told how Jesus is at the center of everything. He said that our old, sinful nature died and was buried with him. When Jesus was resurrected, we were also raised to life, spiritually speaking, but now we have a new nature—a divine nature.

Then he starts chapter 3 by saying, "Hey, taking into account everything I'm saying about Jesus, about grace, and about your new nature, here is what you need to do."

I love how Paul puts the ball in our court: "So, have you been raised with Christ or not? Yes or no?"

"Well, yes."

"Are you sure? You don't sound sure."

"Yes, I'm sure. I have been raised."

"Okay, you've been raised with Christ. Based on that fact, then, seek those things which are above."

In other words, make sure you don't base your obedience on anything other than the finished work of Jesus. Don't strain and stress trying to be perfect in order to earn God's forgiveness. You have a new nature; you are a new person now.

The passage I quoted above uses an odd word to describe Jesus. It says he *sits* in heaven. Sits? He is seated? Lounging with his feet kicked up and a cold drink in his hand? Shouldn't he be pacing the sidelines, yelling at his team to run the play, make the pass, beat the opposition?

Standing looks like action. Urgency. Activity. Jesus should be standing.

But Jesus is sitting.

Sitting is the position of ruling. Jesus is not on his feet. He is not walking around, stalking around, pacing around. He is not biting his nails. He is not sweating.

Jesus is sitting. He is relaxing and he is chillaxing. He is in heaven, and all is well. All is finished. He sits there at the right hand of God, the Bible says, and he laughs at his enemies, and he makes the entire earth his footstool.

If we would center our lives around the reality that Jesus is sitting in heaven, it would affect our Mondays.

The main position of a believer is not walking. It's not pacing. It's not marching. It's not sprinting madly from one activity to the next.

It's sitting. When we were born again, we were called to rest in his finished work.

God is telling us, "Just sit down."

And we're like, "No, God, I got this."

"Sit down."

"But I've got to do—I've got to go—"

"Sit down."

When you wake up in the morning, or when you are working hard at school or sports or music or whatever you love, or when you start to stress about your future—remember to sit down. Remember to center your life around the reality of Jesus. Remember, it is not by your strength, your power, your ideas, your education, or your talent. It is the work of Jesus.

It's Who I Am

The devil would love for us to believe that sin is not completely defeated, that somehow our particular sin slipped through the cross, and even Jesus could not kill it off. So now we're stuck with it. It owns us. It defines us.

The devil is a liar. Sin is defeated. God is for us, Jesus is with us, and his grace is sufficient.

At some point in our lives, we will sin again. And chances are, it's not too far off. But Jesus knew that, and he saved us anyway. In one moment of grace and faith, he forgave every sin you have committed, are committing, and will commit.

Here is a thought that blows my mind: God sees imperfections in me that I don't even see, and he is not stressed about it. He is not planning to work on some of those areas for another thirty years. I'll be sixty-five years old, and one morning God will say to me, "Judah, here's an area we are going to start working on now." And in the meantime, he's not frustrated with me.

He's not stiff-arming me when I try to draw close. He's not locking me in my room so I don't infect someone else. He is telling me that he is proud of me, that he is pleased with me, that I am amazing.

> God SEES imperfections in ME that I don't even see, and HE is not stressed ABOUT it.

We get in such a hurry to make ourselves better because we think that as soon as we do, God will love us more.

But he will never love us more than he does right now. He will never accept us more than he does right now.

God is not in a hurry to fix us. Our behavior is not his first priority. We are his first priority. Loving us, knowing us, encouraging us, protecting us. Those are his top goals and his main concerns.

Our fight against sin is noble and good, but make no mistake: we are not fighting to be forgiven. We already are forgiven. We are just learning to live that way.

In the passage that I quoted from Colossians, Paul says we are to strip off our old nature and put on a new nature. In other words, stop acting like who we are not and instead act like who we are.

It is exhausting to act like we're somebody we are not. Yet that's how we often approach God's commands.

Popular opinion says holiness is hard. Godliness is hard. Giving is hard. Compassion is hard. Telling people about Jesus is hard. But not if it's who I am. All of a sudden I just get to be me. That's not so hard. I can do that.

Often we tell ourselves, *All right, you selfish human being, go love somebody for Jesus today.* And we reply to ourselves, *Okay, that's not who I really am, but I'll try. I'll put on a smile, but I don't want to.*

For some reason, we tend to think that "being a Christian" means "being what I'm not." But that's not true.

Jesus gave me a new way to be human. At the core of my being, I am holy, righteous, godly, compassionate, generous, loving, and sensitive. I have a new nature, and it mirrors the God who created me.

> All of a
> **SUDDEN** I
> just get to be
> **ME.** That's not
> so **HARD.**

God doesn't keep a list of things we did wrong. As far as the east is from the west, the Bible says, that is how far God has removed our sins from us. That's a poetic way of saying infinity. He does not remember them. When God sees us, he does not see a sinner. He sees a saint.

This is who we really are.

Really.

I'm not saying that to trick you into feeling better about yourself. It is not something we say to make ourselves feel better about sin or excuse it. It is the good news of grace.

Sometimes the things we do wrong seem so big and immovable that we think, *This is who I really am. This is the real truth.*

What I really am is bad. What I really am is unholy. What I really am is selfish. What I really am is a liar. What I really am is a negative person. It's in my family. It's my nature. It's my tendency.

So we sin. And we hate it. And we try to fight it, but it's as if we are fighting ourselves.

> The **REAL** me is the **RIGHTEOUS** me, and that is **MORE** real than sin could **EVER** be.

Yes, these sins are real. But they do not define us. Anger, bullying, meanness, evil words—this is not who we are. We have to view those things as aliens, invaders, parasites. They are not part of God's creation.

The real me is the righteous me, and that is more real than sin could ever be.

To save everyone, God became man in the person of Jesus. In the process, he redefined what it means to belong to the human race.

Jesus came to show us a new way to be human.

Talk About It

1. We don't have to act like someone or something we're not. What would you do differently if you knew no one expected you to be any certain way?
2. Have you ever thought that "who you really are" is not so great after all, or even downright bad? Is that the right way to think? How can you change the way you think?

3. What is your "new nature" like compared to your "old nature"? If your old nature was to be greedy, what's the new? Or if it was dishonest, what's the new? What new things can you thank God for?

JESUS IS

My goal in this book has been to help you see Jesus for who he really is and to understand what that means for your life. It is a reflection of me too, and the way Jesus has transformed me. I am more in love with Jesus than ever before. I am more excited about preaching the gospel than ever before.

My prayer is that the love of Jesus will get you excited, that it will change your life and bring joy to your every day. There is nothing like it.

This is just the beginning. I'm convinced that the love of Jesus and the beauty of grace are so massive, so huge, that we will spend a lifetime discovering them.

If certain topics in this book have struck a chord with you, I encourage you to respond. That might mean getting connected to a church or youth group near you that will help you grow in Jesus. It might mean slowing down and spending more time letting Jesus love you. It might mean doing some things differently.

If I could leave you with one thing, it would be this: don't let anything stop you from getting right with God. No matter what you might have done, no matter who you are, it's never too late for grace.

The Bible says that salvation is a gift. It's free. We don't need to clean up our act before we approach God. We don't need to make a sacrifice or pay for our sins. We receive forgiveness by faith, which just means we choose to believe that Jesus died in our place.

I know it sounds too good to be true.

That's why it's called grace.

And that's who Jesus is.

Acknowledgments

Thanks, Jesus.

Thanks, Chelsea.

Thanks, Nuggets (Zion, Eliott, and Grace).

Thanks, Dad.

Thanks, Mom.

Thanks, Family.

Thanks, Friends.

Thanks, Church.

Thanks, Hillsong.

Thanks, Thomas Nelson.

Thanks, Esther.

Thanks, Justin.

Thanks, Sean.

Thanks, Andrew.

About the Author

Judah and Chelsea Smith are the lead pastors of the City Church in Seattle, Washington. Judah is a well-known speaker at conferences and churches around the world. His funny yet meaningful messages open up the meaning of the Bible and show people who Jesus is in their everyday lives.

Prior to becoming the lead pastor in 2009, Judah led the youth ministry of the City Church for ten years. He has authored several books and is a popular voice on Twitter (@judahsmith).

Judah and Chelsea have three children: Zion, Eliott, and Grace. Judah is an avid golfer and all-around sports fan. He believes the Seahawks are God's favorite team, and the fact they won the Superbowl in 2014 is proof that he is right.